# Teaching Students to Self-Manage in the Classroom

## Strategies that Promote Wellbeing and Resilience

ROB STONES

# OTHER BOOKS BY ROB STONES

## The Leader-Mind Equation:
Mindful Choices for Effective Leaders

## The Tao of Team in Practice:
A Treasury of Activities for Forming
and Sustaining a Highly Effective Team

## Minding the Gap:
Choosing to Thrive in an Uncertain World

## The Window of Certainty:
Defining what Matters in your School
Exploring the Difference it Makes
(*with Judy Hatswell*)

## To purchase these books:

Within Australia, please visit Rob's website
www.futureshape.com.au

For orders outside Australia, visit any major online bookseller.

# Teaching Students to Self-Manage in the Classroom

## Strategies that Promote Wellbeing and Resilience

# TEACHING STUDENTS TO SELF-MANAGE IN THE CLASSROOM

## Strategies that Promote Wellbeing and Resilience

First published in 2024.

Author: Rob Stones

Editor: Valerie Stones

Cover Design: Kellie Stones

Image Design: Rob Stones

Image Creation: Rob Stones, Kristin Copson

ISBN: 978-0-646-89317-4

This book is dedicated to the memory of the late
Murray Kitteringham

Murray was a friend, colleague, and an inspiration to many.
A ground-breaking educator, he transformed Sir Joseph Banks
High School through his warmth of personality, infectious
enthusiasm, and passionate dedication to
enhancing the lives of young people.

Almost the last conversation I had with Murray, shortly before his
untimely passing, was about how to expose more teachers to the
strategies that promote a culture of wellbeing in any school.
"You should write a book about this" he told me.

It has taken me a while, but here it is at last.
This one is for you Murray!

*Index of Sections*

*For a more detailed index, refer to Appendix 1*

# What if?

Just two words: opening the doorway to opportunity.

*What if* we began to say aloud what all teachers know in their hearts: that 'the carrot and stick' approach encouraged by behaviourist psychology does not help in the classroom. It's not just that we don't have a big enough stick or juicy enough carrots: the problem is that student motivation is much more complex than that. Even if the stick were big enough, we would simply teach children to be afraid of sticks - and very few people thrive on a diet of carrots!

*What if* we acted on the belief that all young people want to thrive? How might our classrooms change if we assumed that when students know better, they will do better? What if we were to give students the tools to control themselves, succeed and be resilient?

*What if* we acted as if our most disruptive students don't want to wreck their own lives: if we looked beyond their impulsive attempts to feel important or avoid the pain of failure? If we interpreted their intrusive efforts as cries for help?

*What if* we knew for certain that our most unlikeable students want to be loved cared for and supported? Every young person, whether they know it or not, needs a responsible adult as a warm but steadfast person who will offer them unconditional positive regard. When a student acts out in your class, what if it is a sign that they have picked you as the adult they need?

*What if* we encouraged our students to be as powerful as possible, to know that they have choices and can learn to make good decisions for themselves? What if all our students knew how to relate well to both their peers and to the adults in their lives and got to practise those relating skills every day?

*What if* we did not fear that things would fall apart without our controlling hands; if we could be confident enough to place control in the hands of the only people who can be in control – the students themselves?

**What if** you have read these questions and are brave enough to look for the answers?

# THE DESIGN OF THE BOOK

This book is designed to be browsed.

**The Prologue and Section One** provide the 'why' of the book, outlining the reasons for initiating a change in your classroom or school culture, with a focus on student self-management.

**Section Two** explains the psychology of internal control, which serves as the psychological foundation for all the strategies in this book.

**Sections Three to Fifteen** offer 101 strategies for teaching and encouraging students to self-manage.

While you're welcome to read it straight through from cover to cover, many teachers may prefer not to do that. The prologue: **'Who this book is for'** and Section 1: **'Why Teaching Students to Self-Manage Matters'** come first. You may want to at least skim these sections.

After that, you can choose to start exploring the **strategies in the remaining sections** or delve into the **theory in Section Two**. Many of the teachers I've worked with like to check out the strategies first and then return to the theory that explains why these strategies work. Others prefer to start with an explanation of human behaviour that demonstrates why the strategies are effective.

In Section Three, there are **Three Essential Foundations** of Student Self-Management:
1. Eliminating Coercion.
2. Developing Relational Trust.
3. Establishing Collaboratively Developed Boundaries.

These three strategies are interlinked and work best if they are implemented together.

# ~ PROLOGUE ~

## WHO THIS BOOK IS FOR

This book is intended for teachers who work with school-age students in primary and secondary schools. It is a practical guide filled with ideas on how to enhance the classroom experience for both teachers and students.

I am a teacher writing for teachers. I take pride in saying that I have been a teacher throughout my entire career, starting as a classroom teacher and later becoming a school Principal and eventually a coach working with both teachers and school executive staff. Teachers are among my heroes and role models. The lives of millions are enriched by the daily enthusiasm and perseverance of teachers.

Because of my deep respect for teachers, I am concerned to know that many of them feel distressed by the daily challenge of managing difficult behaviour in the classroom. In many cases, this weariness is unnecessary. There's a better way to work with children than engaging in a daily battle for control.

Teaching itself isn't stressful. When students manage themselves, teaching and learning become joyful. It's the management of students that causes stress, both for the teacher in the classroom and the school as a whole. Attempting to control the behaviour of young people introduces distress into the world of education.

When I began working as a teacher, I was taught that we could control children's behaviour using a 'carrot-and-stick' approach. The external control 'theory' of human behaviour that guided our approach was based on observations of rats in mazes or the salivation patterns of tethered dogs. We learned to 'reinforce' behaviours we approved of by giving rewards, and to 'extinguish' poor behaviours by imposing punishments.

Sadly, not enough has changed. The language of external control and the controlling practices that are aligned with that language are still common. Although we know so much more about human behaviour and the science of the brain than we did fifty years ago, many teachers still depend on punishment and reward.

Until the 1980's, external control theory was used to justify the use of 'the cane' or to make misbehaving students write: 'I must always do what my teacher tells me' a thousand times. "Spare the rod and spoil the child" was a popular aphorism.

Since that time, technology has transformed the world. We can now teach a student on the other side of the world, and easily access research that was once locked away in books or academic papers. Social expectations have evolved as well. It is no longer acceptable to hit a child. Meaningless punishments are frowned upon. Despite these changes, most schools still use student management programs based on the outdated behaviourist psychology of the 1970's, but without the draconian punishments that used to be common.

We've changed the names of these programs. We used to call them discipline programs, then student management processes, and now we often label them as well-being programs or use other euphemistic names. Regardless of the terminology, they usually boil down to 'methods for adults to control students'.

The problem is that these discipline programs are misguided. Trying to control other people, whether they are small or tall, presents numerous problems wherever it's attempted. Imposing external discipline is frustrating because it means working against the natural inclinations of other human beings. We are inherently wired to learn self-control, not to be controlled by others - not even by our teachers and parents.

> Day after day, our classrooms are still filled with commands and threats. Damien, a twenty-six-year-old teacher temporarily working as a barista, shared his frustration with the language he felt trapped by when managing a room full of ten-year-old students.

"Susan, please take your seat."

"Michael and Jaimie, stay in your seats."

"Everyone, please take out your reading books and turn to page 34.

"Alex, don't forget your book again."

"Susan, please stop that behaviour. Your name's going on the whiteboard."

"You two will be staying in at lunchtime. It's fair; I gave you plenty of warning."

"Class, please copy what is on the board while I talk to Susan."

"Alice, leave Jaimie alone. Don't argue; I saw what you did."

"Stop that, please."
"Susan, I saw that. Go to the office to see Mr. Thompson."

Damien might not return to teaching. The frustration of attempting to manage his students' behaviour exhausted him, and his initial enthusiasm for the profession faded into cynicism. Like many struggling teachers, he believed he needed more 'tools' to do his job better: tools such as more effective punishments, or stronger executive intervention. He sometimes blamed the problems on the students and sometimes on the system, not realizing that the external control he was using wasn't the solution; it was the problem.

Every human is born with an innate inclination to detect and resist external regulation, including the imposition of another person's will. Since we are social creatures, our survival instinct is adapted to detect and resist threats from other people. We all have an aversion to threats to our self-esteem, autonomy, social relatedness, and our sense of fairness. Our brains automatically protect us from these threats.

Moreover, we have a genetic need for personal power and autonomy. Seeing ourselves as significant and successful is crucial, and acting from our own free will is ingrained in our being. We thrive when we feel in control and when we act willingly. Self-determination is part of our genetic makeup.

The children in our classrooms inherit these human tendencies. That's why they can be challenging to manage, especially when they don't understand that the teacher's intentions are designed to empower them and help them thrive.
**When they feel pushed, they push back.**

The following pages are for teachers who want to bring about change by modifying their approach: teachers who are willing to challenge traditional methods of managing students because they realize that these methods may be causing the problems which they and their colleagues face.

Instead of continuing to do the same things and expecting different results, I invite you to engage with the biological predispositions of your students to help them learn to self-manage. It's a significant paradigm shift.

Einstein is reputed to have said that we can't solve a problem with the same level of thinking that created it. We become trapped by assumptions that are so ingrained that we don't realize they are there. Allow me to share a personal example:

Like so many school leaders, I often focused a large proportion of my time and energy on finding ways to support the students who were struggling and whose behaviours in the classroom interfered with their learning. I reasoned that these students needed more help. It was frustrating work because many of these students seemed to self-sabotage, no matter how much help we gave them.

11

Then came a day when a wise and experienced teacher asked me a crucial question: "Why do we devote so much energy and attention to the 10% of students who are not taking responsibility for their behaviour?"

I offered a glib answer: "Because we can't ignore them; they're there!"

"No, you're not understanding me, Rob," he responded. "The other 90% are there too. Currently, the 10% who cause problems receive 90% of our attention. Imagine what would happen if we were to spend a proportion of that time and energy on the students who are willing to say: "I want to be part of the solution."

This insight and the persistence of teachers who believed that we needed a different way of working led us to introduce a radical 'leadership' program. We invited every student to participate, and two hundred applied, including many we considered 'problem students'. It was controversial, but no one was refused entry to the program, not even those who had shown very little responsibility in the past. We deliberately tutored all those students in self-management and gave them real responsibilities.

**We changed our paradigm**, and the school's culture shifted. Almost all the students in the program flourished and demonstrated real leadership. While challenging students didn't disappear altogether, there were now fewer of them, and their behaviour was influenced by the leadership around them. Focusing on nurturing responsible behaviours instead of dealing with irresponsibility led to a significant reduction in disruptive behaviour.

Experiences like this challenge our beliefs and assumptions and align with the message of this book: Most young people can learn to manage themselves when given the opportunity and taught the skills. They are genetically and neurologically predisposed to learn self-control. As teachers, we can stop the daily struggle for control and use our knowledge of the human mind to teach our students to self-manage effectively. This is a new formula for many teachers, but it can bring joy back to our work.

## ~ SECTION 1 ~

### WHY TEACHING STUDENTS TO SELF-MANAGE MATTERS

Most children work responsibly in the classroom most of the time. If they are reasonably successful with their schoolwork, or if they have learned the habit of compliance, they will follow classroom routines and go along with what their teacher wants them to do.  They are the majority of the students in our classrooms.

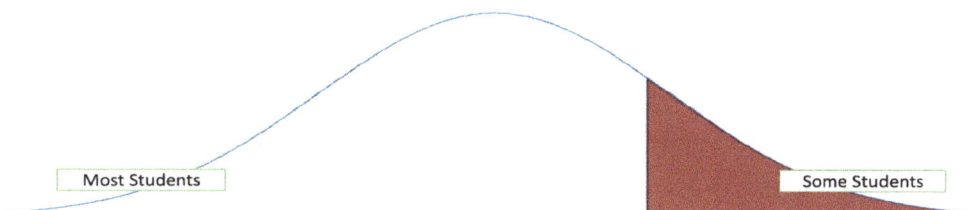

Most Students                          Some Students

However, a proportion of students are not doing well in school. They respond defiantly to the instructions and commands of their teacher and become disruptive in the classroom.  These are the children who interfere with the learning of others and whose influence on the classroom culture increases resistance and frustration. Many teachers tell me that the proportion of such students is growing.

Yet this minority of students, the students who often sabotage their learning and the learning of other children, are following the genetic dictates of their biological selves. The way that they behave is predictable. When they feel they are failing in the classroom, they defend themselves rather than surrender. When they see the classroom as a place where their self-regard is often threatened, they hear potential danger in their teacher's tone and language, even when none is intended. The primitive area of their brain sends signals to the emotional brain to ready itself for combat or escape. As you will see in the next section, this is exactly what the brain's defence system is designed to do. One of the chief functions of our 'crocodile brain'[1] is to alert us to the danger of invasion or oppression.

Now, of course, teachers have no intention of activating defensive behaviours in these students. However, the teachers' intentions are not always obvious to the students. Unless they are deeply trusted, their attempts at classroom control are easily misinterpreted. When a student is not doing well in their studies, and especially when their social behaviours have not yet matured, they intuitively conclude that the classroom is a dangerous place for them. It can be a place where they don't fully understand when their awkward attempts to 'fit in' or to be noisily important are met with threats, and where pain is used to control them[2]. In this perilous context, when they hear commands and threats, or experience punishments for non-compliance, resistance is a predictable form of self-protection.

Compounding the issue is the social context of the classroom. When students choose inappropriate ways of fitting in or feeling powerful, there is an audience for their responses. Their behaviour may begin from craving more attention or seeking identity within the classroom group, but it easily evolves into a public power struggle with their teacher. It is so much more challenging to manage a student when he or she is playing in the theatre of the classroom!

None of this is what teachers want. Almost all of us have only noble goals for our students. Yet we increasingly appear wedged by a context in which we are expected to manage student behaviours, but the available management tools are failing us: where the traditional tools of behaviour management exacerbate our difficulties.

---

[1] The brain stem is evolutionarily primitive. Often called the 'reptilian brain', it looks after our autonomic functions and looks out for danger. I like to call it 'the crocodile brain' because it is fearless and dangerous to those in the vicinity when aroused.

[2] Very few teachers would say that they intentionally impose pain. However, if they are attempting to control using punishments, pain is what they are inflicting. The external control psychology with which punishments are justified is based on the pleasure and pain principle. Pleasurable rewards are given to encourage, and painful punishments are imposed to deter.

The way out of this conundrum is to understand that the theory of external control that underpins traditional classroom management is not fit for purpose. The stimulus-response practices around which most behaviour management policies are constructed are at odds with how the mind works. Rewards and punishments, gold stars and detentions, only work with children who are pre-disposed to be compliant. The 'carrot and stick' approach backfires with resistant students because the teachers who rely on them have no recourse when punishments don't work - except to inflict more punishment! Taking a failing strategy and doing it harder is a commitment to Einstein's parable of insanity.

Notice that attempting external control helps nobody. Compliant students fare little better than their resistant peers with the traditional regime. They can be successfully manipulated by rewards, but the long-term consequences for them may be worse than for the defiant children. An overwhelming accumulation of research[3] shows that students who learn to dance to the tune of external motivations rather than their internal incentives can suffer throughout life from a craving for external validation.

There are proven alternatives to the traditional controlling approach. Teaching students to self-regulate shifts the power dynamic in the classroom. The teacher can stop relying on the primitive imposition of pleasure and pain to tap into the students' inherent capacity to self-manage. Most students will choose self-control over being controlled **if they know how**, and if the expectation of self-control is embedded in the classroom culture. The reason that many schools do not see evidence of students' capacity for self-regulation is that they don't systematically develop it. Because they have not been taught how to manage themselves, young people are as stuck in the traditional approach as their teachers. They can't do better because they don't know better!

The tragedy is that there actually is a better way! There are brain-compatible ways of working with young people, strategies that teach them to understand and manage their minds. By basing their actions on the psychology of **internal control**, teachers can manage themselves in a way that will create a classroom culture that encourages

---

[3] For example: Alfie Kohn's 'Punished by Rewards', and the huge body of research by Edward L Deci and Richard Ryan that is available at 'www.selfdeterminationtheory.org'.

self-control. They can themselves learn and also teach the students how their own minds work and how to use this mental capacity to self-regulate.

**Self Regulation = Better Choices**

Teachers can make these changes without surrendering their authority in the classroom. They can be authoritative[4] without being authoritarian[5], and assertive without being controlling. This way of working is far less stressful and more satisfying than adopting the traditional approach.

This book offers teachers many strategies with which to navigate this alternative pathway – a wide range of practices for creating productive classrooms in which children behave responsibly. These strategies for creating classrooms in which students manage their behaviour are based on cognitive psychology, **the psychology of internal control**. This explanation of human behaviour and motivation is supported by:
- Evidence from cognitive psychology.
- Recent insights about the neurobiology of the brain.
- Research from the 'Self-Determination Theory' community.
- Research by the dynamic communities of neuroscience.

The underpinning explanation of how humans are motivated and why they do what they do is explained in the next chapter.

Remember that this publication encourages you to choose your preferred exploration. At any point, you can go to the strategies that interest you instead of reading straight through the book. Then, if you need more explanation of why some strategies are important, come back to the theory chapter,

---

[4] Authoritative: self-assured and reliable.
[5] Authoritarian: dictatorial and bossy.

# ~ SECTION 2 ~

## CHOICE THEORY: AN EMPOWERING PSYCHOLOGY

There are many explanations of how humans are internally controlled. The explanation used in this book is derived from Choice Theory©, as developed by Dr William Glasser. However, similar theories include Self-Determination Theory, Cognitive Behaviour Theories and Positive Psychology in all its forms. All internal control psychologies **rejec**t the idea that our control system is outside us. Although all of them agree that we do respond to the world around us, we are controlled by what is inside us.

What Choice Theory and the other theories of internal control explain is that we are all individuals who are attempting to look after ourselves in environments over which we have only a little control.

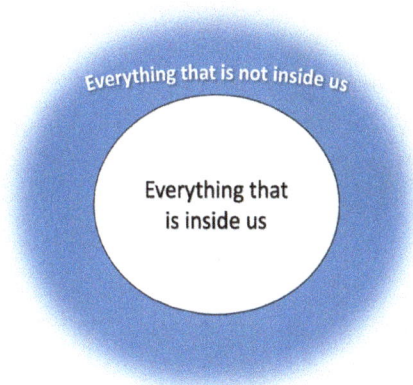

Everything that is not inside us

Everything that is inside us

We can learn how to control what is inside us. We have no direct control over what is outside us. It follows that the only person we can actually control is ourselves. Although we can learn how to connect with and influence the people in the world around us, we can't control them because they are not within the compass of our internal control system. Similarly, we can't be controlled by what is outside us. Although we are affected by people, or by circumstances and events, we can make our own choices about how to deal with them.

Dr William Glasser, the originator of Choice Theory, was primarily a practitioner rather than a theorist. He worked out his 'practice' in the context of working with teenagers in the California prison system (at the Ventura School for Girls). The strategies that he developed focused on teaching young people to take responsibility for their lives. His methods were spectacularly successful in helping irresponsible young people, who were imprisoned because of their criminal behaviours, learn how to manage themselves to become socially responsible and effective citizens. He developed Choice Theory to explain how his methods work.

## A BRIEF OVERVIEW OF THE THEORY:

Our internal control system works like this: We compare our perceptions of the world, both what is outside us and what is inside us, to how we would like things to be.

We then choose actions to bring the world we perceive closer to the things we want. One way of showing this in a diagram is:

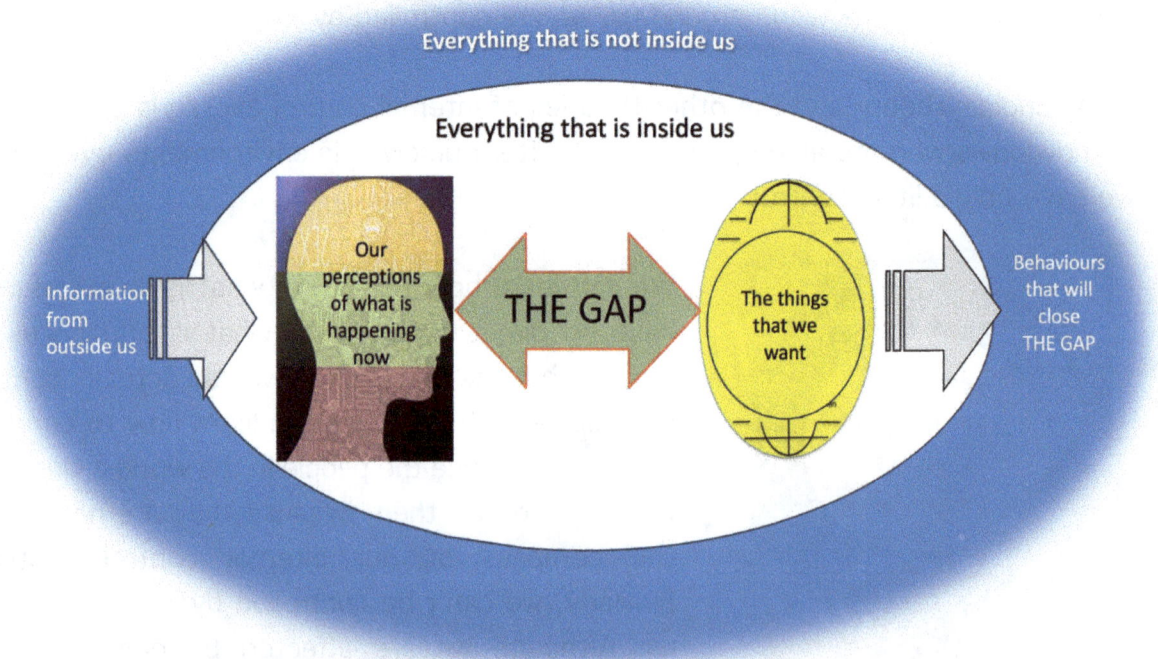

Everything that is not inside us

Everything that is inside us

Information from outside us

Our perceptions of what is happening now

THE GAP

The things that we want

Behaviours that will close THE GAP

The diagram below simplifies this even more: the three main activities of the mind are perceiving, comparing, and acting.

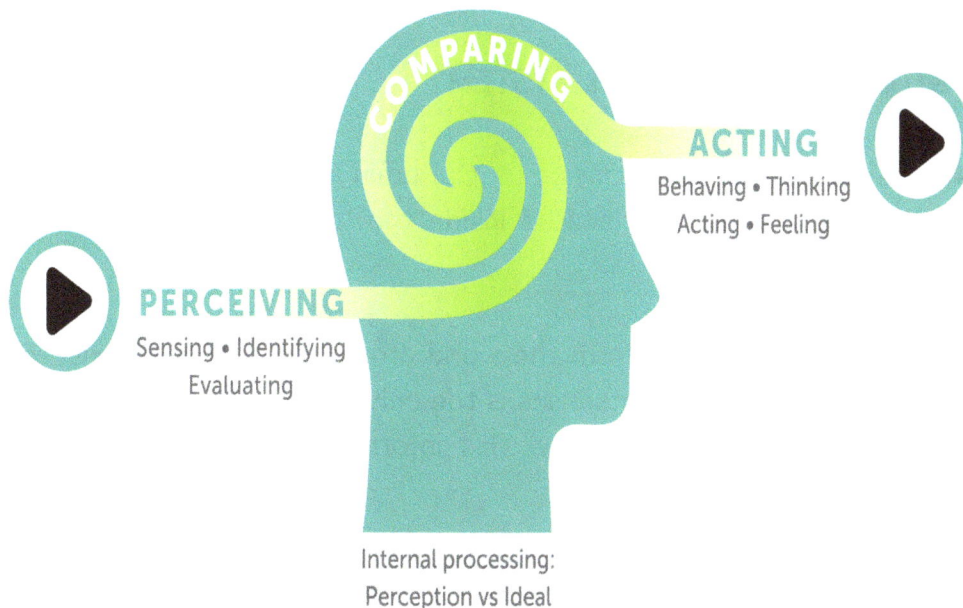

COMPARING

PERCEIVING
Sensing • Identifying
Evaluating

ACTING
Behaving • Thinking
Acting • Feeling

Internal processing:
Perception vs Ideal

Young people who are choosing inappropriate actions to get the attention or sense of control that they want are doing their best with their own control system. They are comparing what they perceive with what they want and choosing the best behaviour they have available to them. From a teacher's point of view, they often seem to choose the wrong behaviours in their attempts to make things better for themselves. They may choose behaviours that damage their relationship with the teacher and harm their own learning and wellbeing. They are nevertheless functioning in the way described by Choice Theory. They want things to be better but they simply **don't know how** to achieve this.

This chapter describes 6 key features of this internal control process. It also explores the implications that each of the six features has for classroom educators:

1. Every Student is a control system.
2. Perceptions are self-created.
3. Everyone has Genetic Needs.
4. An understanding of how Brain and Mind work together.
5. Motivation.
6. The 4 elements of Behaviour.

## EVERY STUDENT IS A CONTROL SYSTEM

This human control system is inside us. Our brain and the neurological network that control our behaviours are located inside the 'bag of skin' that we identify as ourselves.

We do take in information from the world around us: we don't exist in isolation. However, information via our senses is the only thing that we can import from the external world. Whether we allow this information to influence our thoughts, feelings and actions is up to us.

Because the human control system is internal, we can't control another person. That truth can seem shocking or false to many people. We become accustomed to talking about 'making' people do things or being 'made' to behave in certain ways. It is language that misleads us. When we make a reluctant choice to comply with another person's will (to avoid conflict or pain or to keep our job), we are still in control of ourselves. We go along with what someone else wants because it seems the best option to us at the time.

Although we can learn to get along with other people and develop social survival skills, when anyone attempts to control us it is more natural to resist than to choose compliance.  The human survival need almost always pushes back against the invasion of another person's will. However, even when we are being coerced or manipulated, giving in can sometimes seem the best option. Most young people can learn to adopt this external locus of control to avoid pain - or because they think it benefits them to do so.

*When teachers use punishments and rewards, they are trying to make use of the brain's preference to avoid pain and prefer pleasure. It seems to work much of the time, which is why it can seem puzzling and leave them feeling helpless when students resist. Yet these students are being true to their biological selves.*

*Because each child is an internal control system, it is more natural to push back against control than to go along with it.*

*We often regard these students as a 'problem'. We easily get into an arm-wrestle with them when they disobey or disrupt the limits that we try to impose on them.*

*However, this is when we come face-to-face with the reality of attempting to manage another person's control system. The only person whom we can control is ourselves. That is why teaching students to self-manage makes so much sense: they are the only individuals who can take responsibility for their behaviour.*

*Children who choose to be compliant and conform to their teachers' expectations can seem to be no problem for us. However, we may be storing up problems for them. Acquiring the habit of an external locus of control ultimately harms them. Students who adapt their behaviours to gain the approval and praise of their teachers can easily become dependent, give up easily without praise and approval, and have lower levels of resilience.[6]*

*If we can't control students, and if we want them to learn to control themselves well, it follows that, as their teachers, we are best served when we both model and teach self-management. This modelling is especially powerful if we explain what we are doing and allow the students to hear and see how we are managing ourselves.*

## INTERNAL CONTROL.2

## PERCEPTIONS ARE SELF-CREATED

The way we take in information from the world around us can easily mislead us. It seems as if what we see, hear and touch is objective and independent of ourselves. It is not!

---

[6] E.L. Deci and Richard Ryan. See numerous articles at selfdeterminationtheory.org.

All perceptions are self-created. Although they may originate from external stimuli, they are translated by the inner workings of our minds. Every piece of external information that flows into our awareness is simply energy in the form of sight or hearing, smell, touch, or taste. This sensory data comes without meaning. We then interpret this energy through the lenses of our own past experiences, the beliefs we have acquired, and whatever we have come to regard as valuable.

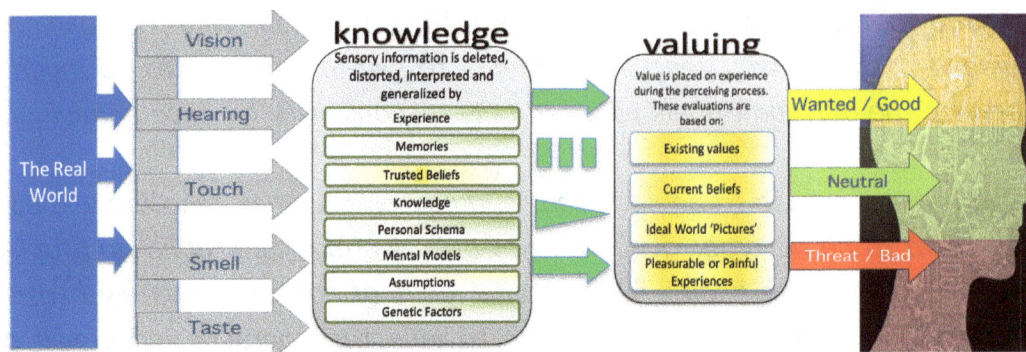

Because no two people have identical experiences, we all have different knowledge and acquire beliefs that can be very different from those formed by other people. For example, the children of loving parents may construct a quite different understanding of the way things are in the world from a child brought up by neglectful or abusive parents.

Similarly, we acquire different values. Children who experience trauma in childhood come to value whatever will keep them safe. They will have defensive attitudes to risk-taking or trust, compared to children from a more nurturing background.

It's as if we all have a personal theatre, viewing the world through internal filters that draw upon and interpret everything we have ever known or experienced. Illuminated by how we have learned to make sense of the world, and focused by the values we have chosen, we interpret everything around us in a highly individual way. Each person's perception is as unique as their own fingerprint, and what might seem clear to one person may appear confusing to another.

*The subjectivity of perception has profound implications for teachers.*

*If we see that a student is 'off-task' and we interpret that as 'misbehaving', the words suggest to us that they are doing something wrong, something that should be corrected. Filtering this perception through our own experience, we start looking for some ways to stop the student from continuing the behaviour. If we are accustomed to using rewards and punishments, it will almost certainly lead us to look for a punishment to 'fix' them!*

*However, If we observe the same behaviour and interpret it as a sign that the student is struggling or confused, we will probably try to help them instead. **The way we interpret things changes everything**.*

*When we stand in front of a class to impart knowledge or to teach a skill, what we are presenting is inevitably filtered by our perceptions.  We usually only teach what we believe will be helpful and beneficial for our students. What the student understands may be very different, adjusted in the intricate maze of **their** perceptual systems. What seems obvious to us can be opaque to them – or have a completely different meaning.*

*For example, many teachers see classroom failure as an inevitable part of the education landscape. Some students fail. It is the norm, so we don't question it. And yet, most of us realise that it is the students who feel that they are failing in school who are most likely to disrupt our teaching.[7]*

*The students who are failing in the classroom perceive their failure quite differently from the teacher. For them the experience is not part of the 'normal distribution' – it is a source of significant pain. Even though the pain seems self-inflicted from the teacher's perspective ('If only they would work harder'!), it does not seem like that to a student who has not yet learned how to connect their behaviours to the painful outcomes that they are experiencing.*

*Of course, we do the best we can to help these students 'keep up' with those in the classroom who learn faster and have a more well-developed sense of how to*

---

[7] Dr William Glasser wrote: "While it is easy to blame a student for not succeeding, there are serious flaws in the school system that make it impossible for many students to feel successful in school." **William Glasser,** 'For parents and teenagers' 2003.

read the social cues of school society. However, we can't take for granted that students who are not doing well will understand our positive intentions or perceive the goodwill that underpins our attempts to help them. Sometimes that is because the student is too immersed in their sense of helplessness or victimhood. Sometimes it is because we forget that we are communicating with a perceptual system that is drawing on very different experiences of the world.

When we want another person to understand the positive intentions of our actions, we have to explain our intentions to them - in a way that the student understands. Usually, we need a good enough relationship with them to encourage them to listen to us and believe us. If we can't communicate our reasons, students are left to make what sense they can of our behaviour in their perceptual system. Knowing this, we must work with children by giving full explanations when we ask them to do things. Expecting them to guess that what we're doing is for their good is not reasonable once we know how perception works. The best teachers I have known and watched always explain **why** they are asking students to behave in certain ways. They remind students: "This will help you to succeed", "What I am asking is what will make things better for you", "I am here to help you, never to hurt you".

We also always need to build specific information about self-management into our teaching. Even the idea that they can be responsible for managing themselves is not necessarily obvious, especially to younger children. Taking some time and care to explain that individuals can only be controlled by themselves will make a profound difference to their perception of what we mean by self-management or self-control.

The other thing that we will need to deliberately teach is self-evaluation. Making judgements about self is central to self-management, but because adults often manage themselves without explaining what they are doing, their self-evaluations are not necessarily transparent to the children. Asking students questions about any dimension of their performance while helping them to explore the evidence for their self-judgments is another crucial step in encouraging students to self-manage.

# INTERNAL CONTROL.3

## EVERYONE HAS GENETIC NEEDS

These needs are fundamental to our existence. We have needs for:

- Relationships - A desire to belong, to be cared about and be loved, to feel accepted and valued.

- Power – The wish to be competent and to be seen as capable and successful, to achieve recognition and significance.

- Autonomy – Wanting to choose our actions willingly, to be self-determined and to dance to the beat of our own drum.

- Learning – Deriving pleasure from learning. When we learn, we are self-rewarded by the release of dopamine, a hormone that produces feelings of pleasure.

- Survival - The need to be safe and certain.

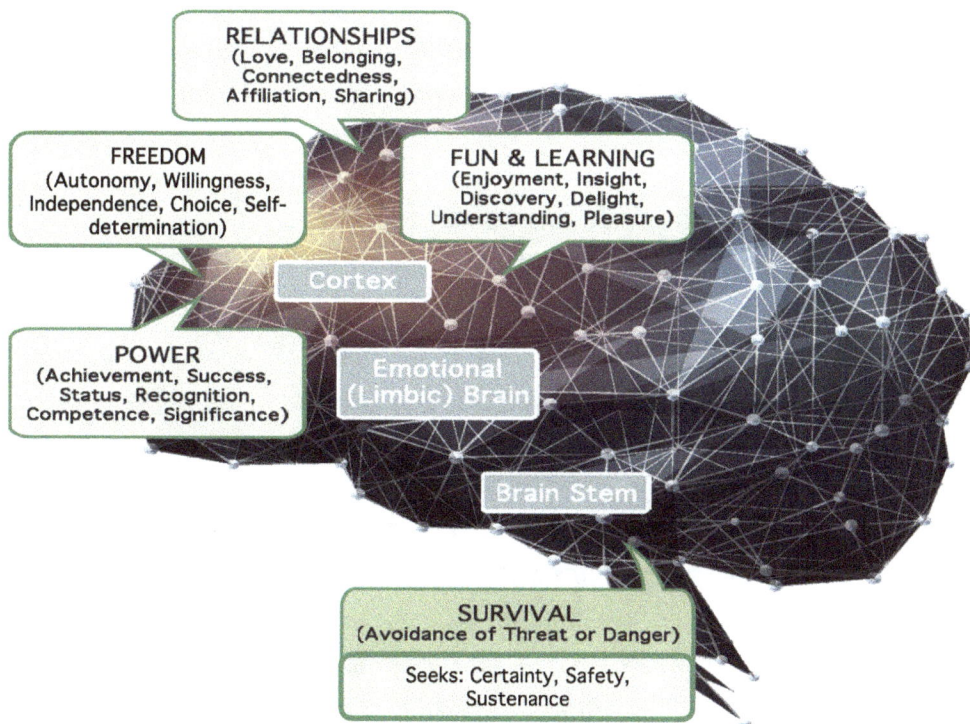

These needs are much more flexible and powerful than detailed genetic programs of more primitive creatures. For example, a turtle is born with the knowledge to break out of its egg, dig through the sand, navigate the beach, and feed itself upon entering the water. In contrast, we humans are born relatively helpless. As babies, we can do nothing without help. However, children possess a remarkable ability to learn and adapt to satisfy their needs, and we all do it somewhat differently.

Learning about these needs is immensely liberating, especially for young people. Because our genetic drivers are not otherwise evident, and many people don't know about them, young people have difficulty understanding their urges and impulses. Understanding the necessities that drive us enhances self-awareness and helps students to make sense of their own behaviours. By teaching students about their needs, we empower them to manage their behaviour. We also provide ourselves with a language to talk about their behaviour in insightful ways.

### 3.1.1

### The Power Need in the Classroom:

As teachers, being aware of human genetic needs, we can understand what is driving our students. So long as students can direct their need for power and recognition through learning, they are often motivated to do well in the classroom.

However, if students perceive themselves as unlikely to succeed academically, or do not yet know how to connect what is expected in the classroom with their increase in competence, they quite often seek power and control in ways that interfere with classroom learning. These are the students who often claim our attention through disruptive behaviours, potentially interfering with their own learning and that of others.

Because the classroom is a public space, the drive to satisfy genetic needs can often distort the behaviours of both students and teachers. A student's behaviour that may begin as attention-seeking or as an expression of frustration can often become a power struggle. When the teacher either does not give them the attention they want, or becomes assertive with them, the student feeds off the social nature of the interaction and plays to the audience. Sensing that their authority is being questioned, the teacher may try to use their position of power to 'shut down' the student. Students take up the power struggle and try to match the teacher's power by clowning, being defiant or sabotaging the teacher's work. The resulting power struggle between student and teacher usually leads to a lose-lose outcome for both.

When we understand that unhelpful ways of seeking power are natural, not simply 'bad behaviour', our perceptions change. We become more focused on helping students to identify responsible ways to be powerful. We can teach them replacement behaviours that are more useful to them than giving up or acting out.

*3.1.2*

### The Relationships Need in the Classroom:

Most students thrive when the classroom is a happy and supportive place for every student. Because all students crave productive relationships with those whom they consider important in their lives, deliberately building such relationships will significantly increase a teacher's influence in the classroom.

Young people who have **not** learned to relate well to others are at a double disadvantage. Although their craving for a good relationship with their teacher is often even greater than that of other students, they have not mastered the relating skills that have been learned by most of the children in their class. They express their need for caring attention loudly and intrusively. Consequently, their teacher may find it more difficult to establish and maintain productive relationships with them.

This is the area where a teacher's misplaced dependence on stimulus-response control really causes harm. Being punished, or being rewarded to control, inflicts harm on the relationship. The student feels that the punishment is a sign that the teacher 'does not like me'. They contrast this with what they perceive as preferential relationships with other students and conclude that they are being treated unfairly. As the relationship deteriorates, punishments and manipulative rewards may be used to correct the student and to 'reinforce' occasional cooperation. These do further damage to the relationship. The damage is being created by coercion, but teachers often try to fix 'the problem' with more coercion!

If teachers work diligently to establish trust through supportive and pleasurable relationships with every student in the classroom, then the environment becomes need-satisfying for everyone. Of course, with some students this is easy. With others, it is very hard work. It requires the teacher's self-discipline to show unconditional positive regard in the face of behaviours that are often quite provocative.

When a student has experienced traumatic events or distressing relationships with other adults in their lives, they are often unwilling to trust their teacher without testing them. Attempting to discover whether the teacher's apparent caring is 'real', students with this kind of damaging history want their teacher to prove that they are really as understanding and warm-hearted as they say they are.

Because we learn best from those whom we trust and respect, the teacher's part in establishing positive relationships (despite challenges presented by students who don't yet have the requisite connecting skills is essential. Relational trust is crucial for the creation of a culture of self-management in the classroom. Challenging as it is, modelling self-control when faced with unfriendly student behaviour may be the most important strategy a teacher can use.

### 3.1.3

### The Need for Autonomy in the Classroom :

The need that inevitably poses a challenge for teachers is the need for autonomy. Sometimes, this is mistakenly seen as simply a desire for freedom, but our craving to be autonomous goes deeper than that. It's the need to feel that we control our actions, to do things willingly rather than unwillingly, and to feel that our behaviours come from our own choices.

In a classroom, an excess of instructions and commands can create resistance because they push against the student's need for autonomy. Providing *opportunities for personal autonomy isn't just about offering choices; it's also about involving children in decision-making, explaining the reasons why students are asked to do things, asking them questions to guide behaviour, and avoiding overly authoritarian commands.*

*Sometimes Choice Theory can be misrepresented as simply always offering choices to students. Although this may be a part of the educational equation, a much bigger part is teaching with such clarity and passion that students work willingly. An autonomous culture is the opposite of a coercive culture. This is the difference between a classroom in which the students work eagerly to satisfy their own needs and one in which the students will not work without incentives.*

### 3.1.4

### The Survival Need in the Classroom:

*It seems obvious that children need to feel safe in the classroom to learn well. However, because humans have been shown to have a need for social as well as physical survival, this need has the potential to interfere with learning. David Rock[8] describes the five dimensions of social survival as threats to the students:*

- *Status or competence*
- *Certainty*
- *Autonomy*
- *Relatedness*
- *Fairness*

*As teachers, we can be especially aware of students who fear that they will seem inadequate or incapable (status), those who are uncertain*

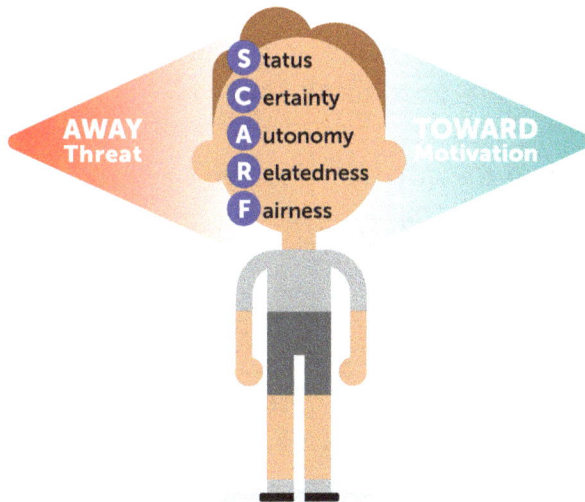

**SCARF Model
of Social Threats and Rewards**

---

[8] David Rock: SCARF 2008

29

*about the reasons why they are learning something, and those who feel that they are not being treated fairly.*

*Among the students for whom safety is critically important are those who are experiencing the effects of previous trauma, often from the effects of ambiguous or chaotic parenting practices. As noted above, these students don't function well if they don't feel safe.*

## THE NEEDS IN SUMMARY:

*Understanding and addressing the genetic needs of students is essential for effective teaching and classroom management. As teachers, we can't satisfy the needs of our students: they are the only ones who can do that. However, we can make sure that the way the classroom is set up provides opportunities for students to meet their own needs. When students' needs are met through positive opportunities, they are more likely to engage in productive learning and less likely to resort to disruptive behaviours.*

*If our goal is to help children become self-managers, to empower them to take charge of their behaviour, encouraging them to make responsible decisions becomes more important than imposing our own will as teachers.*

*When we encounter a child struggling in their studies and displaying irresponsible behaviour, simply telling them to stop won't suffice. This is because the drive for need-satisfaction is an inescapable feature of the human control system. Students are compelled by their nature to keep seeking need-satisfaction. As teachers, our role is to help students find responsible ways to satisfy their needs. Often, this means first identifying behaviours that are not appropriate, and then teaching new behaviours that will satisfy the related need.*

# INTERNAL CONTROL.4

## UNDERSTANDING BRAIN AND MIND

### BRAIN

Every child (indeed every human) is both mind and brain. These are not different entities: they are the two 'voices' of our internal control system.

Think of the **brain** as the automated dimension of our control system. Each human brain contains 86 million specialised nerve cells (neurons). As we learn, countless clusters or 'schemas' of neural connection are formed in the brain. If a sequence of connections leads to pleasure, the brain 'learns' the sequence and automatically connects this sequence, forming a 'schema' that is easily called upon when we want to repeat the experience.

This automation is a crucial aspect of human learning. We don't want to relearn a behaviour every time we need it, so our brain organizes these neurons into efficient patterns, often referred to as 'habits'. The more we use a sequence of behaviours, the more they become automatic.

The habit brain is generally good for us. We rely on the brain's capacity to automate our actions. The patterns of neural connections that we accumulate make it easy to repeat what we have learned.

But the 'habit brain' can be bad for us. It is easier to use the existing neural connections in our brain to do what we have always done, instead of making the effort to create a new behaviour.

When teachers begin to teach students to self-manage, instead of imposing external discipline, the change is initially difficult for both teachers and students. This way of doing things is different from the habits that have been learned in the 'traditional' classroom. The new learning takes effort and has to be repeated and practised before it becomes effortless for them all. This is where the work of the **mind** comes into play.

## MIND

What biological neuroscience has revealed is this: activity in the brain generates bodily sensation that gives rise to consciousness. This enables the electrical and chemical energy from the brain's unconscious activity to be transformed into conscious awareness: into symbols, images, and language. The result of this awareness is that we have personal access to some of what is going on in our brain through thoughts and feelings. The mind can then steer the brain into places where it would not naturally go.

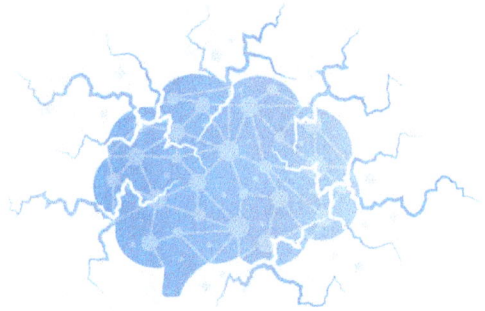

The brain may resist acquiring new behaviours because they require effort. "This is too hard," we hear children say. As teachers, replacing long-practised habits takes a lot of determination. However, the mind can override this natural resistance when it understands the importance of the new learning. Through the activity of mind, we can learn from the past and project the present moment into the future.

*Because our conscious thoughts can modify the activity of the brain, children can learn to do something that goes beyond the normal formation and habituation of neural pathways to gratify an immediate need. **They can acquire the capacity to delay gratification.** Teaching this crucial life skill is one of the most important things teachers can do for their students.*

*The brain naturally leans toward instant gratification; when it wants something, it wants it immediately. This is why many children can be impulsive and find it challenging to commit to something that doesn't provide instant pleasure. Encouraging young people to persevere with a task until they achieve success assists them in acquiring the persistence needed to delay gratification. We can help them to understand the importance of working persistently towards a goal or achievement that may not be immediate.*

*Until children learn the concept of delayed gratification, they tend to become impatient with sustained effort. This poses a potential pitfall for teachers. When we observe children struggling with delayed gratification, we might be tempted to introduce temporary rewards such as gold stars or treats to motivate them to continue working when the learning gets challenging.*

*However, research[9] suggests that using extrinsic rewards in this manner will interfere with the healthy development of delayed gratification.*
*Extrinsic rewards distract children from the sustained effort of working towards a goal. Instead of focusing on working for intrinsic long-term satisfaction, through mastering a new skill or achieving new insight and understanding, children may become distracted by the promise of short-term rewards.*

*Gold stars, merit certificates, or other extrinsic rewards disrupt the normal process of learning to delay gratification. Instead of the intrinsic reward that accompanies success after sustained effort, children transfer their efforts to the accumulation of short-term inducements. Consequently, as they grow into young adults, many of them acquire the habit of prioritising short-term gratification over developing the self-discipline and self-control needed to work through challenges until success or mastery is achieved.*

INTERNAL CONTROL.5

# MOTIVATION

Choice Theory provides a straightforward explanation of how motivation operates in our lives.

---

[9] E.L. Deci and Richard Ryan. See numerous articles at selfdeterminationtheory.org.

We remember and store away experiences associated with the pleasure of satisfying our needs. When our needs are met in very satisfying ways, we store these significant memories and experiences as a sort of mental treasure.

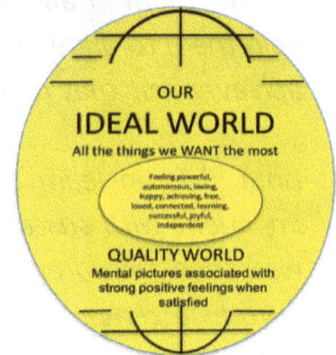

William Glasser described these highly valued experiences as the 'wants' in our 'Quality World'. This accumulation of satisfying experiences is what we constantly seek and strive to achieve.

Our experience tells us that if we can experience the 'wants' in our 'Quality World' or 'Ideal World' we will be happier and more contented.

Our minds and brains continuously compare our current experiences with these idealized memories. We're constantly evaluating the gap between how things are now and how we'd prefer them to be.

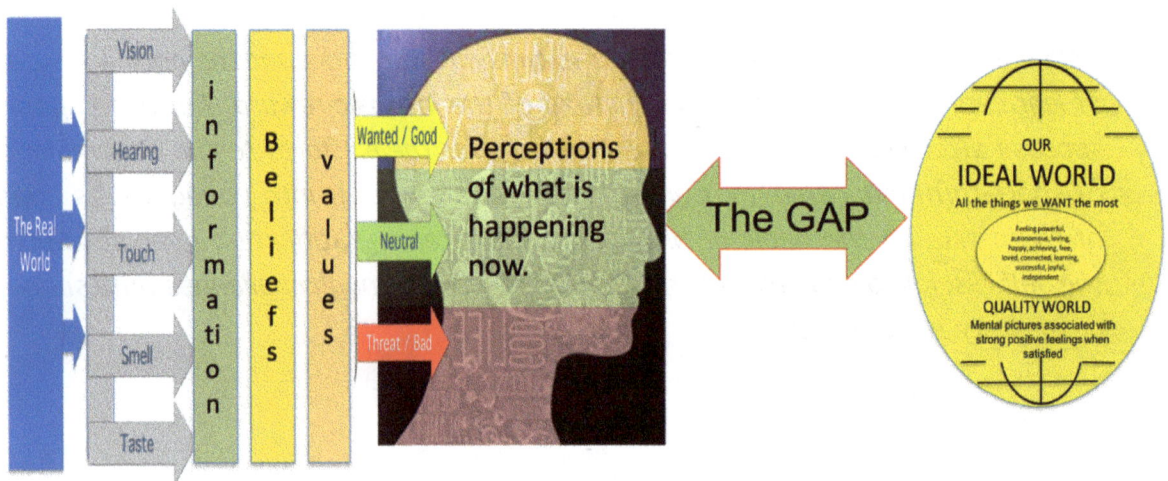

We do our best to close the gap between the two. This process is at the core of what we typically call motivation – our reasons for doing what we do.

When the gap between our ideal world and our present perceptions is small, our motivation may not be very intense. However, if there's a significant disparity between our current reality and our idealized vision, our motivation to act becomes stronger. In psychology, this disparity is known as a 'frustration signal'. When things don't match up to our idealized expectations, it drives us to take action to make improvements.

34

For teachers, these insights have significant implications. Children who have experienced numerous successes in the past are likely to be highly motivated, both in school and in other endeavours, because they associate pleasure with their accomplishments.

On the other hand, students who have encountered few instances of success, particularly in an academic setting, may lack those rich mental images of satisfying success. Instead, they may have learned to seek pleasure in alternative ways. As teachers working with such students, it is vital to assist them in finding ways to experience the joy of success. Without these positive images of success, a student's motivation to succeed in their schoolwork is likely to remain low.

If our positive motivation is not working, we turn to our more primitive motivational system: we behave in order to avoid pain. Positive motivation is known as 'approach' motivation: attempting to accumulate need-satisfying experiences. The alternative is 'away from' motivation: attempting to avoid what we perceive as painful. If what happens in the classroom causes pain and distress, it is natural for students to avoid it.

## INTERNAL CONTROL.6

### THE FOUR ELEMENTS OF BEHAVIOUR

To develop control of our behaviours, we all have to learn how to manage the four elements of our behaviour, or as Dr Glasser characterised them our 4 'wheels'.

Dr William Glasser made a significant contribution to our understanding of self-control by comparing the four elements of our behaviour to the four wheels of a car. Think of the front wheels as our thinking and actions and the back wheels as our feelings, emotions, and physiological state

When we are not happy with our circumstances, we choose actions which we hope will change our situation. When what we are experiencing does not match what we want, we can plan and carry out actions that improve what is happening.

In addition, our thoughts can influence our perceptions of what's happening. Because our perceptions are always interpretations, we can question them, especially when our perceptions of ourselves are negative.

Both thinking and acting behaviours are powerful because they can bring about changes in our lives. When we face challenges or failures, we can plan and use better strategies, practise the new behaviours, and then reflect on what's working and what isn't.

Understanding that they are the agents of their own thinking and acting behaviours is crucial for children. It means that when things don't go as planned, they learn that they can take steps to make the situation better. Even if their choices are limited, there are always goals they can set, plans they can make and actions they can take.

When children learn about the car, they acquire these tools of self-control.

Of course, we also have 'back wheels' which represent our emotions and physiological states. Emotions like joy or sadness can either energize us or drag us down. Emotions are closely tied to our physiological state and level of alertness.

One of the important things that we can come to understand about the back wheels is that they are not as easy to manage as the front wheels. They give us information about how things are going for us, but we can't steer with them. We can't change our emotions by an act of will, which is why we often speak about being 'in the grip' of a negative emotion.

However, all our behaviours are integrated. Dr Glasser called them 'total' behaviours. If we change one of our behavioural wheels, they all change. We all know that our negative physiology changes if we exercise strenuously or dance to upbeat music. When our physiology changes, so do our emotions and our thoughts.

*Teaching children how to shift from their 'back wheels' to their 'front wheels' is crucial, as it is easy to get stuck in negative emotions. By teaching students how to make this shift to the front wheels and offering them strategies to move from negative emotions to productive behaviours, we help children become more self-controlled.*

*One thing to remember is that we can only choose behaviours that we have learned! At each stage of development, children have acquired a set of behaviours which they use to navigate life. If these behaviours are ineffective, they can't be expected to change unless we teach them alternative behaviours - usually ways to acquire more productive actions. Simply telling students to stop a behaviour isn't effective; they need help to replace their un-useful actions with more suitable ones. We can all change our behaviours if we have other behaviours to choose from. The wider the repertoire of behaviours that students can draw upon, the more likely it is that they will manage themselves well.*

*Teaching students the car metaphor provides them with a language and thought process to help them manage their minds. When they are **feeling** frustrated, they can't easily 'stop' the thoughts that are discouraging them, but they **can** learn to* *focus their **thinking** on something that they can do – and, even more powerfully, take new **actions** that will help them to adopt a more useful total behaviour.*

*As teachers, when we notice that a significant number of students in the class seem listless or lost, we can animate their physiology with energising games, provide them with challenging problems, or change their sitting to walking, stretching or even dancing. When they return to the reading or thinking that we want them to do, the change in physiology will make a profound difference.*

# SECTIONS 3 to 15

## 101 STRATEGIES FOR TEACHING STUDENTS TO SELF-MANAGE

The one hundred and one strategies in Sections Three to Fifteen are practices that support the students as they learn to self-manage. They are organised by theme rather than in any order of importance or effectiveness:
- The strategies in Section Three establish the foundation of a classroom culture in which students can learn to manage themselves.
- The next dozen or so strongly support the foundation strategies in Section Three
- There are sections on interventions and TIME-OUT strategies to use in the teaching moments when students are not behaving responsibly.
- There are useful elements of the theory that will help students understand themselves and each other.
- There are teaching and self-management strategies for teachers to apply to themselves.

These strategies are focused on many dimensions of self-management. Some of them fall into the domain that we might describe as 'self-discipline', but others are about control of learning and ways of learning from mistakes.

Many teachers tell me that they are already using some of these strategies, but that they are not always used systematically to promote student self-management. However, when teachers accumulate a substantial suite of these strategies - and intentionally use them to teach students to take responsibility - their students begin to see the world with new eyes. Instead of expecting to be controlled, and feeling relatively helpless compared to their teachers, young people become accustomed to becoming collaborators in their own learning and can take charge of their own life.

## FOUNDATION STRATEGIES

As illustrated by the cartoon below, the change from a traditional classroom where the teacher takes responsibility for controlling the student to a self-managing classroom is a journey. For some teachers, it involves simply enhancing the practices that they already use and adopting the additional strategies suggested in these pages.

## TRANSFORMING YOUR CLASSROOM MANAGEMENT CULTURE

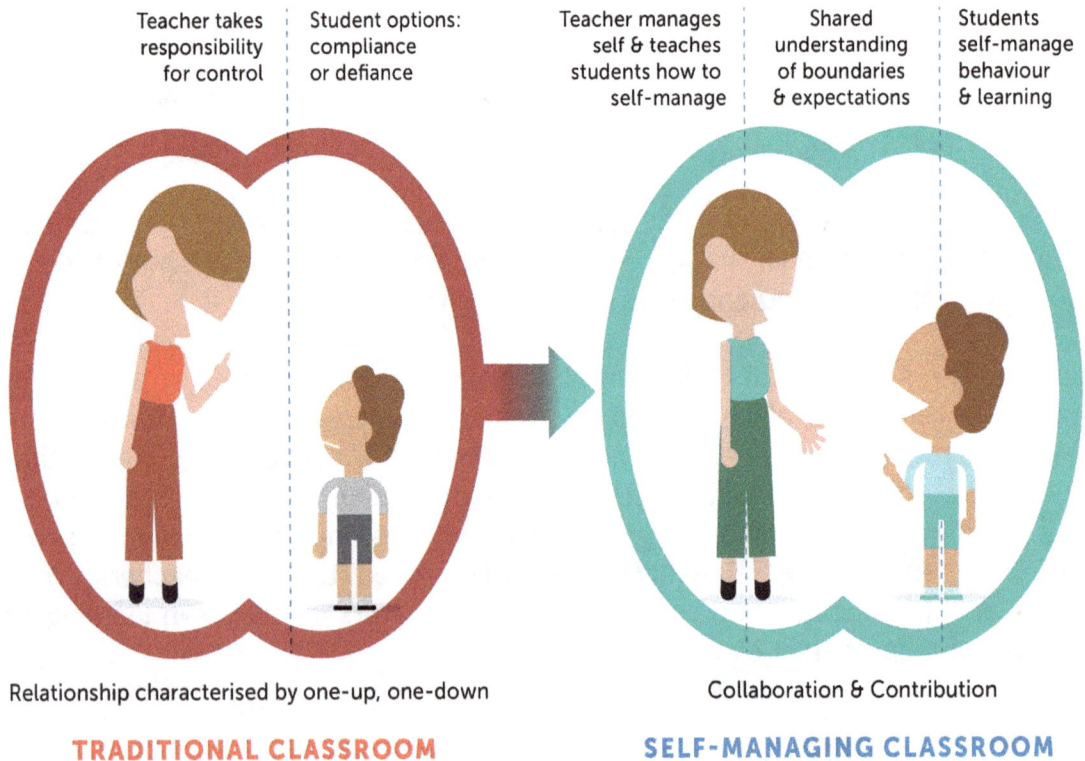

| Teacher takes responsibility for control | Student options: compliance or defiance | Teacher manages self & teaches students how to self-manage | Shared understanding of boundaries & expectations | Students self-manage behaviour & learning |

Relationship characterised by one-up, one-down

**TRADITIONAL CLASSROOM**

Collaboration & Contribution

**SELF-MANAGING CLASSROOM**

These teachers can add these ideas to build the clarity and confidence that students need to manage themselves responsibly. For others, it may be a journey of many steps, beginning with these foundations for creating an environment where self-regulation becomes the norm. Each strategy builds on others as the changes are made and students begin to understand what is expected of them, and to develop the skills and knowledge that they need to manage themselves.

A colleague who was discussing these strategies with me observed that all of them require significant self-management by the teacher. She was right. It is as true of teachers as it is of their students that the only person whom they control is themself. If we as teachers want our students to take control of their behaviour, then we will have to take control of our own!

Malcolm Fidgeon, one of my early mentors, told me nearly 50 years ago: "Your students will learn more from who you are than from what you teach them."

That piece of wisdom has come back to me like an echo at every stage of my life as a teacher. It is embedded in Ghandi's provocative challenge to 'be the change we want to see in the world'. John Maxwell[1] modified an original quote by Theodore Roosevelt when he wrote: "Students don't care how much you know until they know that you care." These aphorisms capture the truth that there is more to teaching students how to self-manage than using strategies. We have to be the calm, confident, self-managing person who embodies the qualities to which we want our students to aspire.

Wherever you are, on the journey from the traditional classroom to the self-managing classroom, three foundation strategies initiate and support the change from teacher control to student self-control.

---

[1] John C Maxwell, American Author and Speaker.

## THE THREE FOUNDATION STRATEGIES:

1. Develop a culture of relational trust.

2. Abandon coercion in favour of assertive practices.

3. Establish collaboratively-developed boundaries.

## The Relationships Knot

These three practices are inevitably intertwined. I call them **'the relationships knot'**. It is difficult to build trust while using coercion. Changing from coercive to assertive strategies depends on having clearly understood boundaries. Setting collaborative boundaries enhances trust, and so on.

As soon as you begin to work on any of these three strategies, the door is opened for the others. For example, asking questions that are non-coercive rather than giving instructions (Section 5) enhances relationships but depends on the existence of boundaries.

## 3.1

☑ **ADOPT**

### RELATIONAL TRUST BASED ON UNCONDITIONAL REGARD

The goal is to develop a relationship with every student based on **unconditional positive regard.**[2]

Almost all teachers know what a powerful influence supportive relationships have on student learning. The challenge embedded in creating relational trust with **every** student is to make sure that our relationship with students is not conditional.

Many children come to expect conditional relationships. The *'if you do as I want I will treat you well'* is the kind of relationship that they often experience from adults, their friends, and sadly often their parents. Conditional relationships are manipulative. They don't contribute to trust.

It is so easy to be kind and caring to students who are pleasant and polite, but to be a little more aloof with and less attentive to the students who are being 'difficult'. It often seems like common sense to ration our warmth depending on how the students act towards us: this is a way of training them to be nice to us.

It's a kind of manipulation of course, but it can seem to be justifiable manipulation.

We would never actually say to students: "I am going to be cold and unfeeling today because you are not being nice to me." – but when that message is communicated by our tone and body language, and especially when it contrasts with the tone and approach used with more cooperative students, then the students pick up the message very clearly.

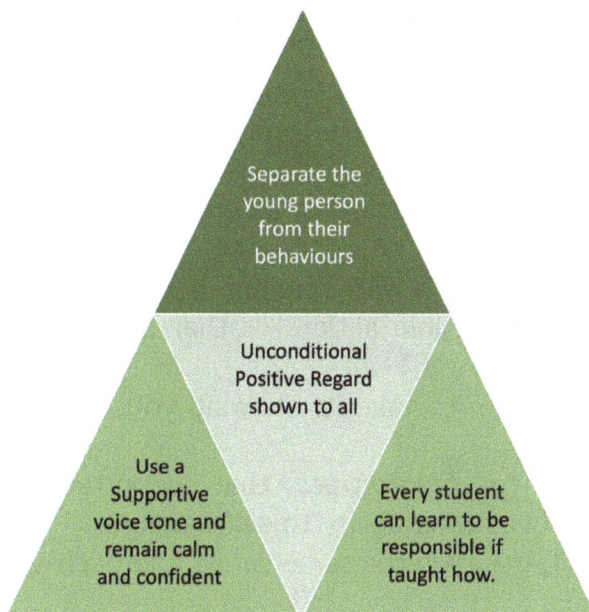

Separate the young person from their behaviours

Unconditional Positive Regard shown to all

Use a Supportive voice tone and remain calm and confident

Every student can learn to be responsible if taught how.

---

[2] This phrase, coined by therapist Carl Rogers, was the key to his person-centred approach to therapy. Organisations such as 'Berry Street' adopt it as a fundamental feature of their approach to young people.

It's important to remember the way in which the perceptual system works. The subtle messages sent by what you do and how you do it, what you say and how you say it, are noticed by all children, but particularly by those who have experienced trauma and unhappiness in their own lives.

Accustomed to being suspicious of other people as a way of protecting themselves from further pain, these children have distrust in their protective armoury. And, of course, these are the students who are usually over-represented in the group that can be difficult to manage.

What else works to develop trust with every student?
The examples on this list are like putting marbles in a jar. The more marbles you accumulate, the greater the degree of trust.

- Be welcoming and caring at every opportunity.
- Give them the gift of your time.
- Get to know them and embrace their differences.
- Listen to what they say and respond so that they know they are heard.
- Say explicitly that your job is to help them to do well and to be happy in the classroom. (This is so easy to implement ,but sometimes teachers forget that students will be appreciative when the teacher says it out loud!).
- Teach relating skills to the whole class: (this does not only apply if you teach Year One. I have spent a great deal of time productively teaching relating skills to 16-year-old students!).
- Give every student an equal opportunity to have your attention.
- Always talk to them in a respectful way.
- Take every opportunity to encourage them with specific recognition and appreciation whenever they take responsible action - rather than giving non-specific praise.
- Give them responsibility and trust them to take it. Showing your trust in them leads them to trust in you.
- Provide them with useful feedback (or *feedforward)* that supports their learning and achievement and improves their ability to self-manage.
- When things go wrong (as they will) maintain the same caring approach and address the problem as a mistake.
- When there are problems, engage more strongly and work it out.
- Never give up!

**Relational trust is built on caring, predictable support for every individual.**

This means doing your best to respond to every student in the same calm and attentive way whatever is happening and whatever they are doing. Yes, it does involve a great deal of self-management, but it pays off. Students will test you. When you pass the test, they will know that they can trust you.

## 3.2

## ☒ AVOID

### AVOID RETALIATION

Avoid basing your treatment of students on how they treat you, or on the part they seem to play in disruptive classroom incidents.

One of the secrets of appearing predictable and supportive is staying calm, confident and in control, and modelling those attributes for the students.

Some teachers behave coercively, believing that being controlling will protect their status and authority. The opposite is true! When we attempt to dominate in the classroom, we invite the students into a power game that damages relationships and interferes with learning.

Like every teacher who ever lived, you will be treated badly by students at times. Your influence and respect will grow if you learn to regard these situations as an opportunity to model the key self-control concept that the only person whom we can control is ourself.

As young people learn how to make their way in the world and work out how to relate responsibly to the people around them, they will make mistakes. Some students learn slowly and repeat their mistakes many times. As the adults in the relationship, we can learn to use the mistakes that they make as an opportunity to teach responsible replacement behaviours.

When things are not going well, teachers should take care not to 'spill the marbles from the jar'. Emptying the jar in anger or frustration may show that we are human, but it will take many hours or days to rebuild trust.

If you avoid the thoughts and actions that can sabotage relational trust, you will find yourself:

- Accepting students as they are and not comparing them with each other.
- Avoiding competitions in which the same students will always be the 'losers'.
- Avoiding sarcasm, criticism and other behaviours that diminish students' confidence and self-esteem.

Perhaps most importantly, become increasingly reflective about your own part in the teacher-student relationship. Dr William Glasser's advice was to take these three steps when things are not going well in your relationship with a student:

1. Set aside some quiet thinking time for yourself. Ask yourself what you are doing to show and explain responsible behaviour to the student. Is the way that you respond when there is disruption helping to make things better in the long term? Is your response improving your relationship with the student or making it worse?
2. If there are some things that you have been doing that are not working, make a promise to yourself to stop doing them. Ask yourself: "What else could I do to help the student understand the behaviours that will help their learning and that will not disrupt the learning of others?"
3. At the very next opportunity let the student know that you would like to work with them to make things better. Be very clear about your role: 'I am here to help you learn and to support you.'

## 3.3

[X] **AVOID**

The transition from using coercion to relying on assertive practices is a difficult one, so please read through the whole of this section with care.

As far as possible, try to **eliminate coercive behaviours** from your repertoire. Attempting to use force to compel students to do what you want them to do will sabotage your relationship with them and will also **create** the resistance by students that can make the classroom a theatre for confrontation.

## Warning – Warning -Warning – Warning – Warning

Please be clear about this step. The very last thing that I am suggesting is a laissez-faire approach. Having an orderly classroom with clear boundaries is critical to creating a self-managing classroom culture.

You will have to set up boundaries with the students and then insist that their behaviour is within the boundaries. There will be natural or logical consequences for students who do not behave responsibly.

However, please avoid the use of:
- Punishments.
- Detentions.
- Threats.
- Rewarding to control.
- Other coercive strategies.

These strategies will damage the trusting relationships that you are working hard to establish. Young people do not respond positively to those who are hurting, threatening, or manipulating them.

**COERCION**

**Coercive practices are attempts to 'make' students do things by imposing or threatening painful deterrents. These include:**

Punishing
Rewarding to control
Threatening
Withdrawing privileges
Imposing detention
Manipulating
Imposing loss of status (levels)
Isolating
Punitively excluding from class
Using sarcasm or 'put-downs',
Brainwashing (using manipulative propaganda)
Emotionally blackmailing
Systematic ignoring
Nagging
Publicly criticising
Suspending
Giving repetitive writing tasks (lines or rules)
Imposing Menial tasks (picking up rubbish etc.)

It's quite common for schools to combine some of the practices above into **systems** such as levels systems, 'Assertive Discipline', PBL (Positive Behaviour for Learning) or the Responsible Thinking Process. There are positive features of these systems, but they are distorted by the coercive practices that are central to all of them.

48

The quadrants below identify the differences between assertive behaviours and other styles of interpersonal communication and classroom leadership.

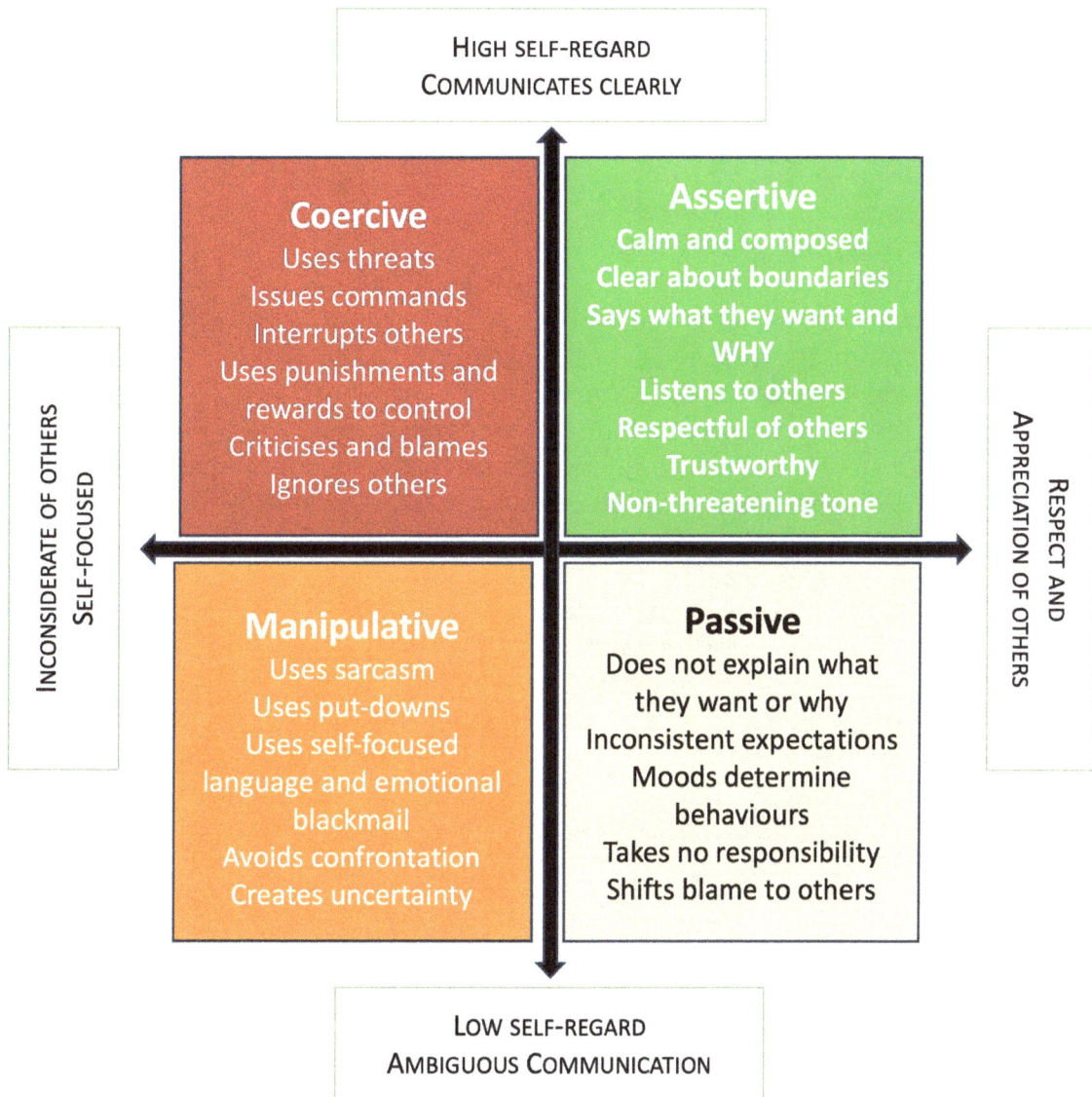

HIGH SELF-REGARD
COMMUNICATES CLEARLY

INCONSIDERATE OF OTHERS
SELF-FOCUSED

RESPECT AND
APPRECIATION OF OTHERS

**Coercive**
Uses threats
Issues commands
Interrupts others
Uses punishments and rewards to control
Criticises and blames
Ignores others

**Assertive**
Calm and composed
Clear about boundaries
Says what they want and WHY
Listens to others
Respectful of others
Trustworthy
Non-threatening tone

**Manipulative**
Uses sarcasm
Uses put-downs
Uses self-focused language and emotional blackmail
Avoids confrontation
Creates uncertainty

**Passive**
Does not explain what they want or why
Inconsistent expectations
Moods determine behaviours
Takes no responsibility
Shifts blame to others

LOW SELF-REGARD
AMBIGUOUS COMMUNICATION

## 3.4
## In place of coercion:

☑ **ADOPT**

### ADOPT ASSERTIVE PRACTICES

**Make sure that boundaries are clear (see next pages).***

Establish the **purpose** of teaching students to take personal responsibility.*

Use assertive practices include:

- **Saying what you want and why.***
- Listening for meaning and acknowledging difference.*
- Using 'I' statements.
- Applying the 'Broken Record' technique.*
- Using 'Fogging' to deflect criticism.*

Give clear instructions in a firm, non-threatening tone.*

Apply natural or logical consequences such as time-out or 'make-up' work - (See the notes on punishments versus consequences below). *

Show respect.*

Respect differences.

Show unconditional positive regard.*

Teaching replacement behaviours.*

Practise unconditional positive regard.*

Negotiate problems.*

Develop Trust.*

Build Capacity.*

Teach inspirationally and enthusiastically.*

Coach and Counsel.*

Flip from negatives to the positive.*

Teaching the 'how' of self-management.*

Use and teaching Connecting Behaviours.*

Tell the students that you care about them.*

Listen.*

Encourage.*

Use Influence and Persuasion.

Replace commands with questions*

Use **'Working it out'** when problems occur.

**Many of these practices are explained in later sections as indicated by a ***

## ☑ ADOPT

### CONSEQUENCES

We are all responsible for the consequences of our actions. Learning that our behaviours lead to outcomes or results is an important part of learning to become responsible and take charge of our lives. When students learn to connect what they do or say with the outcomes that follow, they understand that they are in control of the consequences of their actions. There is still much that they can't control (other people and events), but they learn that taking responsibility is the way to get what they **do** want and avoid what they don't want.

Some consequences are natural. When we take risks we sometimes get hurt. When we don't plan where we are going we might get lost. These consequences follow naturally enough from our actions. Nobody else is involved.

Logical consequences are different. When we are unkind to our friends, our friends avoid us. When we don't do the work in class, we are expected to catch up in our own time.

In school, it is mainly **logical consequences** that are used to help students learn how to be responsible. In every case, the connection between the behaviour and the consequence must be clear. A consequence is a result of something that the student has done (or has not done). A consequence is predictable and is mostly in the control of the student.

> It is easy to confuse consequences with punishments. A colleague of mine once worked in a school with a 'levels' system. Being demoted through the levels was punitive. However, the teachers were encouraged to say: 'You are choosing 'Level 4' when a student was being punished by losing privileges or sent to detention.
>
> This is simply wrong! The students may have been choosing irresponsible actions or careless mischief, but they were **not choosing 'level 4'**.

The intention of applying a consequence is that it leads to learning. A consequence helps students learn how to connect an outcome with a behaviour. The consequence aims to help the student to be and to feel more in control of their own life. An effective consequence is predictable and provides the student with an opportunity to rectify or remediate the result in some way.

A consequence should always apply if a student is deliberately outside the classroom boundaries or school boundaries. Note: If there is no clear or identifiable boundary, then any inappropriate behaviour is an opportunity for a discussion with the students and for establishing a new boundary.

So, let's summarise:
- Consequences help the student connect their behaviour with what follows.
- They are intended to inform and assist the student.
- They help the student to be more in control.
- They are predictable.
- They are strongly related to clearly identified and understood boundaries. That is why the Boundaries chapter that follows is inextricably connected with effective consequences.

There are essentially four cues for a logical consequence:
1. You break it, it's your job to fix it or to clear it up.
2. If you damage a relationship, it is your responsibility to repair it.
3. When you abuse a privilege, you lose it until you recommit to and demonstrate responsible behaviour.
4. When you act impulsively or disruptively you will be invited to take TIME-OUT if you do not immediately take remediating action.

In practice, when the boundaries are clearly defined, a student who is behaving irresponsibly, or whose actions are outside the boundaries, is initially asked:
"Is what you are doing inside the boundaries we agreed?"

As students begin to understand these questions, processes are used to either:
- Quickly agree to a replacement behaviour.
- Take the student aside until the matter can be discussed.
- Remove them from the classroom temporarily until one of the many 'working it out strategies' can be used. (For more details go to the chapter 'Working it out: when things go wrong').

**ALL CHOICES HAVE CONSEQUENCES**

## 3.6
**☒ AVOID**

### PUNISHMENTS

Punishments are logically and psychologically different from consequences.

A punishment is a painful experience imposed by one person on another for one of three reasons:
1. To deter them from doing something.
2. As retribution for something they have done.
3. As revenge for some distress felt by another person.

In schools, punishments are usually advertised as deterrents. However, they are often perceived by the student as 'revenge'.

The idea that punishments are effective comes from stimulus-response psychology which is an outdated and inadequate explanation of human behaviour. The simple idea that comes from S-R psychology is that we hurt children to deter them from behaviours we do not approve of and give them a pleasurable reward to encourage them to do what we want. In S-R theory, punishments are regarded as essential tools for anyone who wants to control another person.

The simple idea seems to work on rats in a cage. It does not work so simply on human children. Humans have complex cognition. Compliance is not their only option when they are faced with a punishment. Anger, resistance, defiance, and resentment are also possible - and very common.

In two of my other books, I have told the personal story of my own experience with punishment. When I

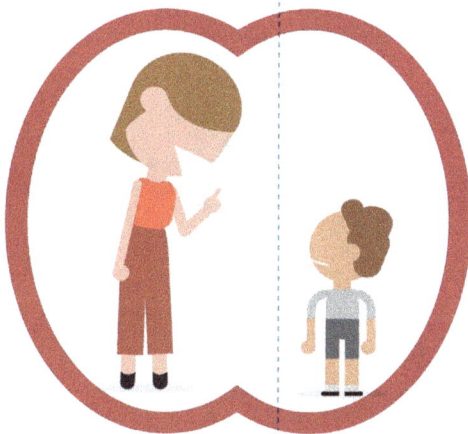

Teacher takes responsibility for control | Student options: compliance or defiance

Relationship characterised by one-up, one-down

**TRADITIONAL CLASSROOM**

was twelve, I was hit with a piece of bamboo ('the cane') every Tuesday for several months. The intention of my teacher (who was following the stimulus-response psychology that he himself had been taught) was to force me to memorise my Latin vocabulary. He believed I was lazy and needed to be deterred from my idleness.

He did not succeed, though he did teach me two things. I learned to hate Latin (an unfortunate consequence as my wife, a former language teacher, often reminds me!). I also learned to despise the teacher for his commitment to keep caning me even though it was clear that I was not going to make any attempt to learn my Latin vocabulary. After a few weeks, the original punishment was increased to three strokes of the cane, and when that did not work either to four!

As the illustration above shows, I had two options: compliance or defiance. I chose defiance!

What my story does illustrate is how dysfunctional using punishments can be. When they are not working as the teacher intends, they will almost always be escalated. Teachers see themselves as having no recourse other than to increase the punishment, even though it is not working. The disconnecting behaviour becomes even more disengaging!

Remember that the change we are attempting is illustrated below:

### TRANSFORMING YOUR CLASSROOM MANAGEMENT CULTURE

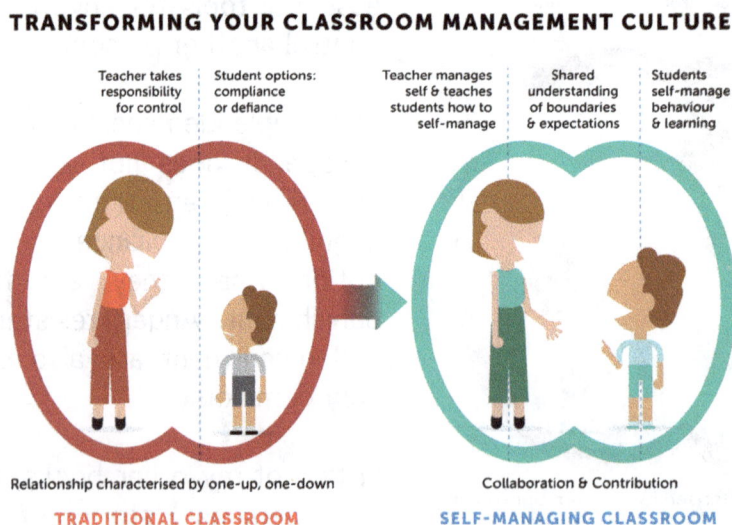

| Teacher takes responsibility for control | Student options: compliance or defiance | Teacher manages self & teaches students how to self-manage | Shared understanding of boundaries & expectations | Students self-manage behaviour & learning |

Relationship characterised by one-up, one-down

Collaboration & Contribution

**TRADITIONAL CLASSROOM**          **SELF-MANAGING CLASSROOM**

## 3.7

☑ **ADOPT**

### COLLABORATIVELY-DEVELOPED BOUNDARIES

There are at least four ways in which to develop boundaries in the classroom: to create limits that will provide clear guidelines for students who are learning to self-manage.

Use one of these practices to replace 'rules' as your way to set classroom expectations. Rules are one-dimensional: they specify what to do or not do (and often contain an 'or else...'), but do not give enough information about the responsible way to behave.

**Boundaries are different from rules**. Boundaries establish ways of distinguishing between what is responsible (inside the boundaries) and what is not responsible (outside the boundaries).

There are several ways in which to set boundaries and I have listed four. All take some time to set up, but they will repay the time taken by the degree of cohesion and certainty that are established in the classroom. In all four cases, once the boundary is established and understood, students will be expected to refer to it as they self-evaluate their behaviour.

Some teachers tell me that the kind of boundary they set is often age-appropriate. The simpler boundary processes such as Your Job /My Job are used for the early years, while the 'Window of Certainty' approach is more appropriate for Upper Primary and High School classrooms.

Notice that all of these ways of setting boundaries are collaborative. They are established in discussion with the young people in your class. They can be reviewed and revised with the class at any time, but any changes should always be made through collaborative discussion.

# ☑ ADOPT

## BOUNDARY SETTING

### Boundary Setting One: MJ/YJ

The simple boundaries activity, often used by teachers, is to establish:
**My job/Your Job** and **Not My job / Not your Job.**

Most teachers who use this approach use the kind of rectangular frame illustrated here. The **My Job** is the teacher list, and the **Your Job** is the student list.

| My Job | Your Job |
|---|---|
| NOT My Job | NOT Your Job |

Through discussion and negotiation, the teacher and the class decide what behaviours should be entered into each of the four quadrants.

The MJ/YJ approach is very useful for making it clear that students are expected to manage themselves.

I was watching a teacher with a class of Year Two students setting up their boundaries while sitting under a tree to shelter from the February sun.

She asked: "Whose job is it to learn?" and almost all the students agreed it was their job. However, whenever a behaviour was suggested for each box she asked: "Who agrees with that?" and made sure that she had unanimous agreement before allocating it. If there were students who did not raise their hand in agreement she used the opportunity for discussion and negotiation. When one student asked: "Is it your job to learn as well?", she paused for a discussion and then agreed with the class that it was important that **she** was a learner as well. 'To learn' went in both boxes.

When she asked: "Whose job is it to control the class?", most of the children said it is **your job**. She shook her head gently and waited. Eventually, she asked: "Whose behaviour can I control?"

After a long pause, a boy said uncertainly: "You can control you", and she nodded in agreement. "I can control myself," she said, "and it is my job to control myself."

Then she continued: "So whose job is it to control **you**?". Some students knew the answer to that question. Their Year One teacher had made it clear that self-control was their job. For other students, it was a new idea, so the teacher took time to explain it until every student agreed that it was **'their job'**.

Later in the day, the class was in the library. At one stage, the noise level rose and the teacher clapped her hands once and raised one arm until she had the attention of the class. She asked: "It's getting a bit loud in here. Whose job is it to keep the library quiet?" The noise level dropped immediately!

**When using MJ/YJ to set boundaries, the questions the teacher might ask are:**
Is that your job?
Whose job is that?
Do you know what your job is?
If that is not your job, whose job do you think it is?

## 3.9

☑ **ADOPT**

## Boundary Setting Two: Above and Below the Line

The second way of setting boundaries is to use one of the variations of above the line/below the line where behaviours that are above the line are responsible and those below the line are not.

| Above The Line |
| :---: |
| Responsible, Cooperative |
| Below the Line |
| Interfering, Disruptive |

The process for setting the boundaries is the same as the one used in MJ/YJ. The behaviours above the line and the behaviours below the line are collaboratively agreed upon by the teacher and class, and thoroughly discussed when there is any vagueness or disagreement.

Some teachers initially include plenty of detail as they construct the **above** and **below** dimensions, although most agree to summarise these in their working document. For example, the teacher and students might agree to combine behaviours such as: 'calling out', talking when the teacher is talking, 'tapping a ruler on the desk', 'distracting another student' and 'making weird noises' as one category of **'disruptive behaviours'**.

**With this approach, questions from the teacher for the student could be:**
Is what you are doing above or below the line?
Are you acting responsibly when you do that?
Do you know what to do to be above the line?

## 3.10
☑ **ADOPT**

### Boundary Setting Three: Inside and Outside

Inside and outside is an enhancement of the previous method but uses a circle instead of a line. It is like a halfway step between methods three and four.

The oval does much the same job as the 'above and below the line' but takes it a step further. It makes clear that the autonomy of the student (the things that they can do freely) is not limitless.

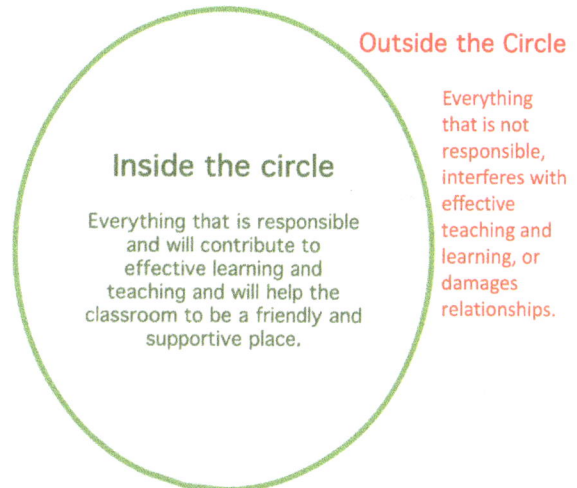

**Inside the circle**

Everything that is responsible and will contribute to effective learning and teaching and will help the classroom to be a friendly and supportive place.

**Outside the Circle**

Everything that is not responsible, interferes with effective teaching and learning, or damages relationships.

While autonomy is encouraged, responsible behaviour is always confined to those things that do not interfere with the need-satisfaction of other students or of the teacher.

As the Inside and outside model is developed collaboratively, it provides a good opportunity for a discussion about 'what is responsibility?'. I like Glasser's definition: "Behaving responsibly is getting your needs met without interfering with the need-satisfaction of anyone else." However, I never impose that definition. I let the class decide - provided that their definition incorporates the idea that responsible behaviour is both looking after oneself and looking out for others.

The kinds of questions the teacher might ask to encourage self-evaluation are:
Is that inside our circle?
Where do you think we should place that behaviour: inside or outside?
Are you inside our boundaries?
Can you get yourself back inside the boundaries?

## 3.11
☑ **ADOPT**

### Boundary Setting Four: The Window of Certainty©

Finally, there is the 'Window of Certainty' process for establishing boundaries. This is a highly effective way of establishing shared purpose and common principles as well as boundaries. It can be used with children of Year 5 and upwards, and of course with adults as well.

Many schools use the 'Window of Certainty' process as a way of developing cohesion between their staff across the school, as well as with class groups.

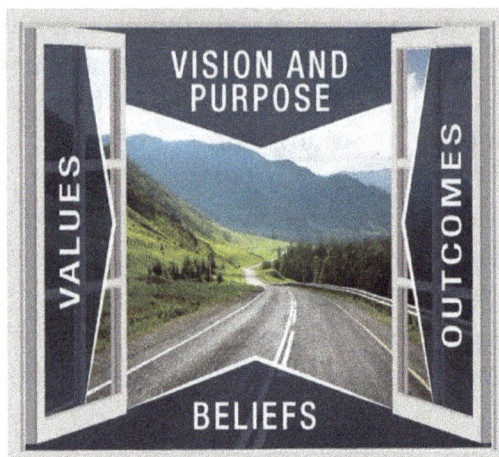

The four 'Frames' of the Window form the boundaries. The Frames are:

**Purpose:** this establishes **'where we are going'** both as individuals and as a class. It describes both personal goals and the explicit improvement agenda that the class or school might be working towards.

**Outcomes:** these describe how success or improvements will be measured. They help to answer the question: **'How are we going?'**.

**Beliefs:** these encourage the class to discuss how they will achieve the outcomes they have set for themselves. Strategies are associated with beliefs (i.e. what do we need to do to achieve the goals we have set for ourselves?). This frame is particularly important because if the class decides, for example, that a belief that they are all internally controlled belongs in this frame, they are most likely to take responsibility for their personal achievements. If they believe that 'asking questions' or 'completing all set work' is crucial for success, they will be more likely to adopt those strategies. The Beliefs Frame answers the question: **'What are we doing to achieve our vision?**

**Values:** these establish the way that the class members will work with each other. Because values are closely tied to behaviours - If I value courtesy I will tend to behave courteously - this frame establishes a mutually supportive class or school culture. The Values Frame answers the questions: 'How will we behave?' or 'How will we treat each other?'.

Spelling out some detail in the Beliefs and Values frames rewards teachers and students who take the time to include all of the things they believe will be crucial to success and wellbeing.

With the 'Window of Certainty' approach, there is no need to list the behaviours that are outside the Window. Everything that is inside the Window and contributes to achieving the goals and outcomes of the class, AND is aligned with the agreed beliefs and values, is acceptable. Anything that is outside any of those boundaries is not responsible.

Self-evaluation questions the teacher might ask include:
Are you inside the Window?
Is that what we believe or value in this class?
Will that belief lead to the best outcomes for you?
How can I help you to get back within the boundaries that we agreed upon?
Is that taking us in the right direction?

*For more on the 'Window of Certainty'© approach go to my website* [www.futureshape.com.au](www.futureshape.com.au) *to purchase my book: 'The Window of Certainty'.*[3]

---

[3] Rob Stones and Judy Hatswell: 'The Window of Certainty' FutureShape publishing, 2016

# ☒ AVOID

## AVOID RULES

Rules are mostly in the form of 'Don't do this' and often include disguised 'or else' threats: (If you break the rule this will happen to you).

**Rules imply morality**. Following the rule is 'good' and breaking the rule is 'bad'. One is right, the other is wrong. These moral judgments are often automatically attributed to the students. 'Good' students follow the rules; 'Bad' students break the rules. These kinds of labels are not useful.

Expectations are a little better if they are framed as positives, but they are also one-dimensional. They give information about what is responsible, but not what will be regarded as not responsible or needing improvement.

Boundaries have a different effect on perception because they are not about right and wrong. They clearly define which behaviours are responsible and therefore encouraged. What is above the line or within the boundary is identified and is used to generate self-evaluation questions:
'Is that inside the boundary?'

This has a very different tone from 'Is that against the rules?'.

# ~ SECTION 4 ~

## THE CLASSROOM CULTURE IS ABOUT TO CHANGE

Making changes by stealth rarely succeeds. Covert changes are sabotaged by the perceptual systems of the young people whom we teach. Because our expectations influence what we notice, students will often not even be aware that you are changing your behaviours and expectations unless you explain what you are doing.

What happens as a result of making your changes secretly is that nothing changes. The students' behaviour will not vary because they do not know that it is supposed to! The teacher's behaviour will tend to return to the previous 'normal' because the students are not engaged with the change.

The way out of this trap is to be intentionally direct and open. Let the young people with whom you are working know **what** will change and **why.**

Once you have asked them to notice that you are making some changes and also let them know that you expect their cooperation, they will become alert to the changes that you are making.

We are changing!

## 4.1
## ☑ ADOPT
### OVERTLY TEACH THAT EVERYONE IS INTERNALLY CONTROLLED

It is important to teach the WHY of teaching students to manage themselves.

Explain to the students that managing themselves and their learning is their job. It is **their** job because nobody else can do it!

Use this **Internal** and **External** image to discuss the difference between what we tell ourselves to do and what other people tell us to do. When the students are very young, you might focus this conversation on how they can benefit from learning from their parents and teachers. As they grow older, the focus will shift strongly to personal responsibility.

Everything that is not inside us

Everything that
is inside us

Students are often not accustomed to thinking that they are in control of their own behaviour, so these are often rich conversations.

You can roll this idea into a conversation about the advantages and disadvantages of being internally controlled.
**Advantage:** You are in charge of yourself. Your choices matter.
**Disadvantage:** No excuses. You can't blame someone else for your behaviour.

**Your job** is to teach, demonstrate, steer them through the curriculum and provide experiences that will help them learn and thrive.
**Their job** is to manage themselves in ways that help them to benefit from your teaching, as individuals and as a class.

Teachers sometimes have misgivings about this strategy. They say to me: "If the students know that I can't control them, won't it compromise my authority?".

The reality is that accepting and teaching that students are internally controlled allows you to be an authoritative teacher rather than an authoritarian one. Students will respect your candour and your authenticity!

Young people already know your limitations as a controller. The students at Bamaga High School where I was the Principal, used to respond to instructions by saying to me: "You're not my boss.". They were right. My relationship with them was grounded in authenticity. We did not need the fiction of illusory control.

As you switch to strategies that support self-management, you can explain to students that you are changing your approach in order to encourage higher levels of achievement, greater commitment to learning and increasingly responsible behaviours, **from and for them**, as a result of this change.

## 4.2
## ☒ AVOID

### ELIMINATE OR DIMINISH THE HABIT OF EXTERNAL CONTROL.

This means giving up bossing, dominating, and controlling your students.
Replace these habits with using your natural authority as the expert teacher in the room.

There is a pragmatic and psychologically important reason for giving up your role as the boss in the classroom. Although imposing your own will on students may be partially successful some of the time, it will always risk the responses of resistance and resentment. At best you will get compliance from many students, not wholehearted engagement.

Even more importantly, **if you** manage the students, they will not need to manage themselves. They will go along when they want to but play the game of 'make me' when they don't. Crucially, they will not make any improvement in managing themselves.

As the teacher, you never relinquish your role in setting boundaries and insisting that students remain within those boundaries. This is one of the key strategies in Section Three. It will always be the teacher's job to be the boundary rider.

However, the boundaries can be set and maintained calmly and confidently when the students understand that they are learning how to take charge of themselves, rather than merely 'doing as they are told'.

You can and should still give instructions (see Section 5.3). Instructions are central to your role as an instructor. Only use them to inform rather than to control.

## 4.3

☑ ADOPT

### SIGNAL FOR ATTENTION

Adopt clear signals to get the students' attention. These signals should not require you to overpower the students by the loudness of your voice or by the use of threats. These should be a combination of sounds, actions and posture that make it clear that you want to speak. They should be taught with a clear WHY: an explanation of your reasons for using these signals instead of shouting.

Examples of sounds that you might use include tapping on a water glass (sounds very 'Rotary Club', but it works!), ringing a small bell, using a chime or tone, clapping your hands three times, or playing the distinctive ringtone on your phone.

ADD to this a physical signal such as raising your hand and ask students to amplify that signal by raising their own hands. Sometimes teachers who use these cues accompany them with a 3-2-1 sign with their fingers.

At the same time, make sure that your physiology expresses a clear message that you are waiting for their attention and expect it!

Whatever signals you decide to use, PRACTISE the signal over and over again with the students until there is no doubt about what you want and the responsible and respectful attention that is expected of them. Don't be put off if the students take time to learn this new less intrusive way of getting their attention. Try to make the practices a game.

I am sometimes told that these 'low-key' signals will not be effective in the robust setting of a public High School: "That's all too subtle for my school", as one deputy principal told me. That was a perspective from someone who has never tried to make this change!

It is one of the many paradigm shifts involved in transforming the culture and expectations of a class or school. The nature of a new model of what is possible is that people have difficulty seeing what they have not experienced. However, without making the change they will never experience the shift.

I have observed teachers in a large high school who were unable to gain the respectful attention of a class of 25 students, however loudly they yelled. Yet, in the same school, a senior student would stand in front of one thousand students at a school assembly and establish quiet within a few seconds by raising her hand, standing tall and waiting expectantly.

## 4.4

## ☒ AVOID

Shouting at or attempting to gain attention in a domineering manner. Although these are common approaches, they are exercises of attempted 'power over', and they usually raise the noise level instead of diminishing it. In attempting to rise above the hubbub of an excited group of students, it is all too easy to add to the noise and escalate it. What is needed is a contrasting sound that can be heard through the voices. It need not be loud to achieve this.

Trying to overpower the students to get their attention is also psychologically and physiologically harmful to the teacher. It increases frustration, raises blood pressure, and quite easily interferes with the teacher's own self-control.

## 4.5
## ☑ ADOPT

### DEFINE RESPONSIBILITY

Adopt a **definition of responsibility** with the students. You can initiate this by drawing their attention to the ambiguous way the word is used. Even young children notice that adults urge them to be responsible without necessarily always meaning the same thing.

With children in the youngest grades, it is acceptable for the teacher to offer a definition of responsibility and then discuss it with the children so that the definition makes sense to them.

With older children, you may be best served by conducting a Classroom Meeting or a Yarning Circle (see Section 6) about the meaning of responsibility:

The 3 steps of a classroom meeting are:
DEFINE. PERSONALISE. CHALLENGE.

**Step 1: DEFINE** responsibility. Accept inputs from all students and continually summarise their responses.

Make it clear that you are not aiming for a teacher-centric definition, but one that works in the adult world as well as in the classroom.

| The Classroom Meeting |
| --- |
| Sit in a Circle |
| **DEFINE** What does this mean? |
| **PERSONALISE** What does it mean to me? |
| **CHALLENGE** How will this challenge us? |

You are aiming for some version of: **'What responsibility means in this class is everyone getting what they need to do well and be happy, _without_ interfering with other people's ability to do well and be happy.'** You will notice that the discussion always trends in this direction.

**Step 2: PERSONALISE** the definition by asking students to talk about what it would mean to them if all students and the teacher behaved responsibly. Look for and encourage responses that note that students will have more freedom if they behave responsibly.

**Step 3: CHALLENGE** the students to think and talk about the difficulties of establishing the expectation that every student is in charge of behaving responsibly and that the teacher's job is not to command them but to ask them: 'Is that responsible behaviour?'.

Take this opportunity to assert that you will be trying hard not to criticise, accuse or evaluate the behaviour of a student if they are not behaving responsibly. Instead, you will ask them to evaluate themselves against the standard agreed upon. Remind them that when they hear: 'Are you behaving responsibly?', it is their cue to make a judgment about their behaviour.

**⌧ AVOID** any reliance on criticising, guilting, threatening, or manipulating the students when they are not behaving responsibly.

When students' behaviour is interfering with your teaching and with students' learning, simply ask:
1. 'What are you doing?'
2. 'Is it responsible?'
3. 'Do you know what you should be doing?'
4. 'Can you do what you should be doing?'

Use a calm, non-threatening tone of voice.

When they begin to behave responsibly, say: 'Thank you', and move away.

## 4.6
☑ **ADOPT**

### SELF-EVALUATION

Throughout the book, you will find examples of students being expected to evaluate their own behaviour, work, and effort. As we make the changes to encourage students to self-manage, it will be important to make clear that you expect them to self-evaluate, and to become increasingly accurate and reliable in their ability to evaluate their own work and behaviour.

Self-evaluation is an essential feature of self-management. Because everyone is an internal control system, we all tend to respond to the need for changes or improvements that come from inside us. We have all experienced this. Indeed, it's such a common feature of experience that we tend to ignore its significance.

When another person tells us we are wrong, or that we should make changes in our behaviour, we don't automatically feel motivated to make changes. In fact, we often resist when we are told what we **should** do. Unless we trust the other person and respect their opinions, then their judgments about what we should or should not do usually fall on deaf ears.

This all changes when we decide that they are right! Who decides? We decide! We form the intention to act or think differently of our own volition. It's from our self-evaluation that we make the decision to behave differently.

Our students **will** self-evaluate. Whether we teach them the practice of self-evaluation or not, they do it automatically. Our job as their teachers is to help them to refer to both internal and external criteria so that their self-evaluation is valid and reliable.

The process that helps a young person's ability to self-evaluate is a cycle. Students refer to the knowledge, intuition, and emotion in their own internal map of how things are. Through thoughtful and respectful feedback, we help them to connect this **internal** map of reality with trusted external sources.
As the two dimensions of this cycle connect with each other, their internal map becomes more informed and their judgments more accurate.

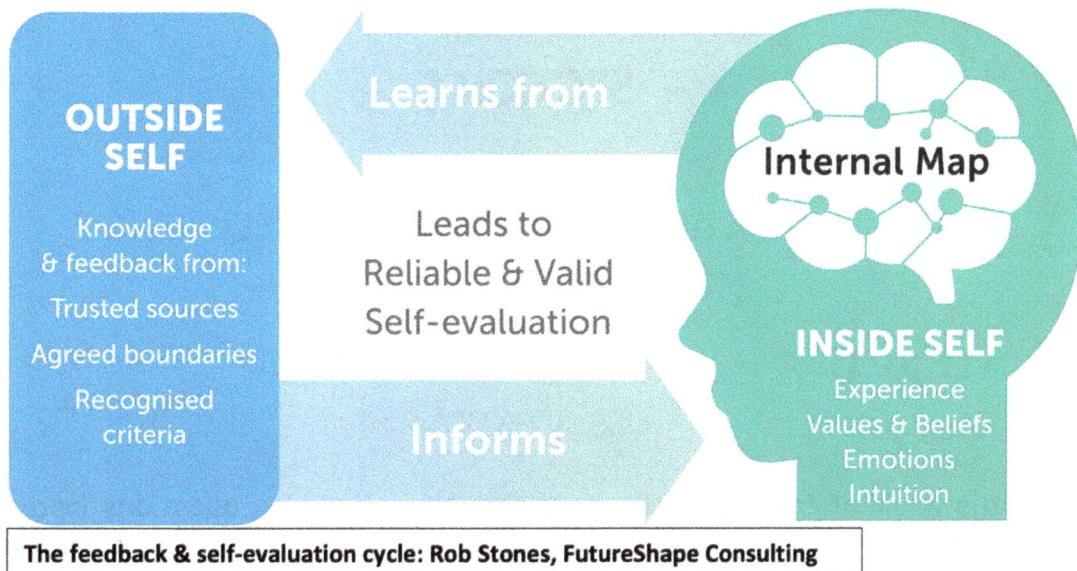

**OUTSIDE SELF**

Knowledge & feedback from:

Trusted sources

Agreed boundaries

Recognised criteria

Learns from

Leads to Reliable & Valid Self-evaluation

Informs

**Internal Map**

**INSIDE SELF**

Experience
Values & Beliefs
Emotions
Intuition

**The feedback & self-evaluation cycle: Rob Stones, FutureShape Consulting**

The other element that enhances a young person's ability to make trustworthy judgments of their own performance and achievement is to ask them self-evaluation questions.

As described in more detail in Section 5, asking questions as opposed to making teacher judgments elicits a young person's own evaluation. The more often these self-judgments are exercised and balanced with external feedback the more informed and accurate the self-evaluation becomes.

# ~ SECTION 5 ~

## COMMUNICATION THAT SUPPORTS WELLBEING

### 5.1
### ☑ ADOPT

#### USE QUESTIONS

Adopt the habit of **talking to the cognitive brain** by using **questions** instead of **commands.** Use questions whenever you intervene in a situation where a 'correction' might normally be used, or an order given.

As shown in the diagram below, how we talk with students in these situations makes a great deal of difference to their responses.

**Read from the top on the left, and from the bottom on the right.**

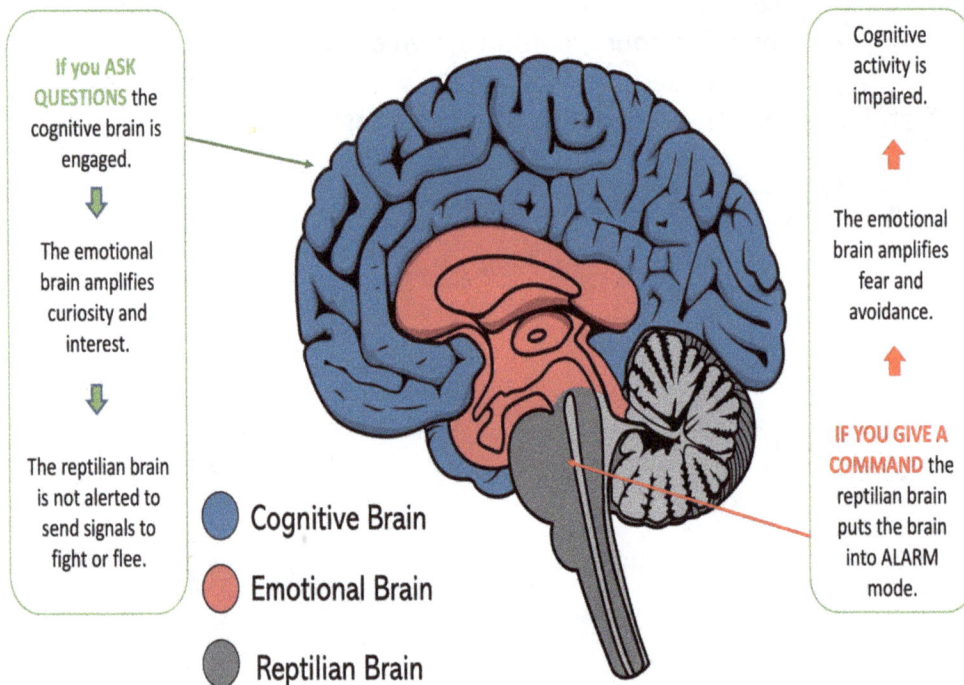

If you ASK QUESTIONS the cognitive brain is engaged.

⇩

The emotional brain amplifies curiosity and interest.

⇩

The reptilian brain is not alerted to send signals to fight or flee.

Cognitive activity is impaired.

⬆

The emotional brain amplifies fear and avoidance.

⬆

IF YOU GIVE A COMMAND the reptilian brain puts the brain into ALARM mode.

● Cognitive Brain

● Emotional Brain

● Reptilian Brain

When we give commands, or issue instructions in a bossy way, the brain's most primitive structures respond. The brain stem, often called the reptilian brain because it is the most evolutionary primitive part of our brain, is designed to look out for any kind of threat. Because commands, especially those given forcefully can be perceived as threats to safety and autonomy, they alert the primitive brain. When we hear a threat, we tend to respond defensively or resist.

Using questions to replace coercive or critical language is a key feature of effective brain-to-brain communication in the classroom. When you ask a student a question, their brain processes your query through their frontal cortex. That is the cognitive control centre of the brain. Questions increase the chances of eliciting a thoughtful response, especially if a self-evaluation question is used.

**Self-evaluation questions** are a special kind of question. Self-evaluation questions invite the student to identify and assess their own behaviour. Self-evaluation questions promote self-management.

When a student is 'off task' or choosing a behaviour that distracts from the learning process, instead of: "Stop that!" and redirecting their behaviour with an instruction, simply ask them to **identify** their behaviour by asking: 'What are you doing?'.

Whatever you hear, follow up with an evaluation question: 'Is that inside the boundaries?' or 'Is that what you should be doing?'.

Because self-evaluation questions encourage students to take ownership of their behaviour, they are the best option for a teacher who wants to both challenge behaviour and **enhance student self-management**. Questions take all the complication out of it. They tend not to precipitate resistance.

It is as easy to ask: 'What are you doing?' and 'Should you be doing that?' as it is to say: 'Stop that and do as I tell you!'.

**[More on Questions in 5.3].**

## 5.2

## ☒ AVOID

### CONTROLLING LANGUAGE

Avoid the habit of using controlling language, or bossing, accusing, criticising, or remonstrating with the student.

In making the change from command to question, what you are attempting is to avoid language and behaviour that implies that you are controlling the student. Replace that language with questions that make it clear that you expect the student to be responsible for their behaviour.

## 5.3

## ☑ ADOPT

### A REPERTOIRE OF USEFUL QUESTIONS

The simple questions used on the previous pages show how **self-evaluation questions** can replace teacher command and control when an intervention is needed. These kinds of questions assist students in learning to manage themselves.

It's important to remember that the control system of every person's behaviour is inside them. Every student chooses a response from inside: from their brain. Whatever questions (or instructions) we give as teachers, the response comes from inside the mind of the young person with whom we are working.

The wider the repertoire of questions you have, the more likely it is that you will have the 'right' question to elicit responsible behaviour from the young person with whom you are working.

The examples in this section are intended to provide you with a stockpile of questions to use in talking with students. Based on Dr William Glasser's 'Reality Therapy'[1] procedures, their intention in the classroom context is not therapeutic. Used as classroom interventions, they are simply very useful questions for helping a student to **identify** and **evaluate** their present actions, and then seek an **alternative** and more useful behaviour.

There are three stages of these questions:
1. What are you doing? (asks the student to **identify** their behaviour).
2. Is it responsible? (asks the student to **self-evaluate**).
3. What can you do instead? (asks the student to identify a **replacement behaviour**).

Using these questions (sometimes only one of them is required) provides you with a quick intervention that enables you to redirect the behaviour of a student in a calm and supportive manner.

Let's embed the questions in three scenarios. The following sequences are all simple situations where a teacher might normally instruct the student to stop their present behaviour and tell them what to do instead. I have colour-coded the three questions to make it easier to follow when slightly different words are used.

Notice that I am assuming that you have begun to adopt the foundation strategies, and explained the changes that you are making (Sections 3 & 4). If you have not made these changes, the students will probably be less than cooperative.

1.
Simon has been explaining a maths problem to his Year 4 class. He gives them some examples to work on and notices that Julie is not attempting any work and is tapping on the desk with her pen.

"What are you doing, Julie?", he asks quietly.
"Nothing", she replies.
"Do you know what I have asked you to do?"
"Do these silly problems", she grumbles.

---

[1] Dr William Glasser wrote 'Reality Therapy' in 1965. It described the counselling processes he used successfully in teaching responsibility to young women in prison. Since that time the processes he developed have been adapted for coaching and teaching in other contexts – especially in school classrooms.

"Do you know how to start or would you like my help?
"I think I know what to do."
**"Thank you",** says Simon as he moves away to another student.


2.
Danielle's Year 9 class is working on descriptive writing. She showed
them a short film extract that depicted two teenagers visiting a big city
for the first time. The task she has given to the class is to choose one
of the boys and describe his reactions to what he sees, hears and feels.

Martin calls out: "This is stupid. Why are we doing this?"
"It sounds like you have an issue with the task. What have you done so
far?", responds Danielle with a smile.
"I just don't get this", Martin responds.
"Have you been able to make a start?", asks Danielle.
"No!", the boy replies.
"Have you chosen which boy to write about?"
"Not yet."
"Would that be the first step for you to take?"
"Maybe"
"Can you make that choice?"
"I suppose", Martin said in a grumpy voice.
"Can you make a start by deciding which boy to write about?", asked
Danielle encouragingly.
Martin grunted. "Maybe."
"Will you start and then let me know if you are still having trouble?"
"Alright."
**"Thank you",** says Danielle as she moves away.


3.
Alison is conducting a demonstration in her technology design class. She
notices that two of the boys keep pushing each other.
She intervenes: "John and Chris, what are you doing?"
"Nothing", they mutter.
"It looks to me as if you are pushing", Alison says: "Who is responsible
for your behaviour?"
The boys look at each other and shrug.
"Each of you is responsible for what you do.", said Alison. "What does
behaving responsibly look like in this situation?"

"We could watch what you are showing us."
"Would that be easier if you moved apart?"
The boys start to separate from each other.
**"Thank you."** Alison resumes her demonstration.

These are very ordinary scenarios, except that the students are now cooperating instead of resisting. However, please notice **what the teachers are doing** and **what they are not doing** to elicit a cooperative response.

- In these examples, the teacher did not **'tell'** the student what to do. As a result, the student has no command to push back against.
- In each case the triple question format was used: What are you doing? What should you expect of yourself? **What else can you do?** The teachers shape the actual question to match the situation but use the same pattern of questions so that these become familiar to the students.
- The exchange between teacher and student is not prolonged. When the teacher hears that the student knows what to do they say, 'Thank you' and move on. There is no prolonged eye contact or controlling body language which would imply controlling management by the teacher.

Of course, any question can be asked in an aggressive or confronting way, and that will change the student's perception of the communication. It will be heard as threatening or antagonistic. However, if the questions are asked in a friendly or inquisitive tone, they usually elicit a thoughtful response.

When you begin to replace commands with questions, it is useful to assemble your repertoire of 'Responsible Self-Management Questions'.

**Remember, when a student is 'off task', or choosing a disruptive behaviour, ask:**

What are you doing? Students must identify and name their unhelpful behaviour.

Is it responsible? (or Is it what you should be doing right now? or Is this what I have asked you to do?). These questions ask the student to self-evaluate their behaviour, such as:

What else can you do? (or What should you be doing? or What could you be doing? What would be a better way to get what you want without disturbing other students / or disrupting the lesson). These questions Identify a **replacement behaviour**.

One teacher in a large Sydney School told me that she was not getting on well with her Year 9 science class. Taking the advice of her pedagogy coach, she wrote down all of the corrective instructions that she used in a single lesson. She was a bit surprised at how many there were!

She then took some time to herself to turn all of these directions into questions and committed herself to using them every time she taught the class. Almost immediately it made a difference!

She expressed surprise at the change, explaining that the class 'felt' easier to work with and students were less disruptive.

"I had to work really hard to remember to ask questions instead of just telling them what to do", she told her coach. "It was worth it though. Lessons with them changed from a constant battle to a much more relaxed and friendly experience."

The list of questions in the table below is intended to help you acquire a repertoire to use in the many different situations that you will encounter with your students.

| What are you doing? | Is it outside the boundaries? * | What else can you do? * |
|---|---|---|
| What's happening? | Who is responsible for what you do? | Can you get back inside the boundaries? |
| What's going on? | Is that inside the boundaries or outside them? | Can you do better? |
| Can you tell me what you are doing? | Is that responsible? | Do you know a more responsible way? |
| Can you describe what you are doing? | Is that OK? | Is there something else that you can do? |
| What is that about? | Are you doing your best when you do that? | Is there a better way? |
| If I was a fly on the ceiling, what would I see? | Is that helping or hindering? | Do you know a better way? |

| Where is this going? | Is that taking you forwards or backwards? | What other options do you have? |
|---|---|---|
| Are you OK? | Will that improve the situation? | Is there a more effective way? |
| What am I seeing? | Is that your job? | Is there anything else you can try? |

\*Notice that the questions in red are all self-evaluation questions, and the questions in green prompt the student for alternative options.

## 5.4
## ☒ AVOID

### AVOID THE HARD STARE

Attempting to stare a student down to dominate them nearly always backfires.

**A glare turns a conversation into a contest!**

Try using the very opposite behaviour. Disengage from eye contact as soon as the student acknowledges that they know what you expect them to do.

Say **'Thank you'** and move away.

When you use this strategy to end a series of questions or an instruction, you are signalling that the interaction is complete. The student knows what to do. The teacher expects that the student has accepted responsibility for taking the action that has been agreed upon. No confrontation is necessary.

In contrast, the hard stare sends a very different message. It says: 'I don't trust you to take responsibility' and 'I am in control, and I will wait to make sure that you are obedient.'

Saying **'Thank you'** and moving away increases the probability that the student will take responsibility. Locking eyes in a challenging way almost always sends the message: 'This is me against you and I am going to win!'.

No strategy is ever 100% effective. You might have to come back to the student and continue the conversation with further questions. The student may choose to escalate the interaction whatever you do. However, as teachers, we are most effective when we use the strategy that is least likely to heighten the sense of conflict:

Say **'Thank you'** - and move away.

## 5.5
☑ **ADOPT**

### GIVE INSTRUCTIONS AUTHORITATIVELY

Although questions are a wonderful tool for teaching students to manage themselves, they can't replace instructions in the teaching and learning process. Giving instructions is central to the practice of teaching. However, when we are teaching students to improve their self-control, it is important to give instructions in an *authoritative* rather than an *authoritarian* way.

Authoritative instructions are clear, reliable, and accurate. The source of their authority is their validity and accuracy. They are **helpful** for the student. Authoritative instructions are given calmly and confidently.

In contrast, instructions given in an authoritarian way are dictatorial and bossy. When you use an authoritarian tone and language, the focus changes from 'helping' to 'managing' and discourages students from managing themselves.

The difference here is in **HOW** instructions are given.

I like this illustration of the difference between a helping relationship and an authoritarian one. Authoritarian relationships are characterised by one-up one-down interactions.

Teaching is a helping relationship but, as described by Edgar Schein[2] in 'Helping', the one-up, one-down relationship is not conducive to the teacher being seen as helpful.

The exaggeration of the power imbalance in this kind of communication replaces the teacher's legitimate 'expert power' with 'position power'.

In contrast, when the teacher presents themselves as an expert instructor, working in collaboration with a self-managing student, the relationship becomes balanced and there is no need for the dynamics of domination.

Being an instructor is one of the behaviours we all need in our role as teachers.
Whether we believe in student-centred learning or more direct didactic forms of instruction, giving the student information (through direct teaching, conducting a demonstration or organising an activity) is always a vital part of the practice of teaching.

I think of instructions as the input phase of the teaching-learning process.
The clearer and more effective the input, the more likely it is that the student will be able to take responsibility for processing their learning.

For a student to self-manage their learning effectively the input (instruction) must inform them about:
- What to do.
- What outputs are needed from them.
- The success criteria (how to self-evaluate their learning).

When teachers want to encourage students to take charge of their behaviour, learning and achievement, high-quality instructional practices are a key dimension of this shift in responsibility.

Students are more likely to behave responsibly if the teaching is meaningful, interesting, and inclusive.

---

[2] Edgar H Schein: 'Helping' Berrett-Koehler, San Francisco, 2009.

This is one of the most powerful reasons to teach students to self-manage. When the students are behaving responsibly, the teacher can focus on teaching. The more effective the teaching, the less likely that students will become bored or restless - or feel that success is unattainable.

## 5.6
☑ **ADOPT**

### USE FLIPPING[3] TO TRANSFORM THE NEGATIVE

Negative comments, especially negative 'self-stopper' judgments, are always unhelpful in the classroom. These can range from 'I can't do this' to 'This is too difficult for me' or 'This is very boring'.

Often teachers respond with reassurance such as: 'I am sure you can' or are challenged by this kind of negativity from the student. However, **hearing a negative expression is an opportunity to discover the positive preference that always accompanies it.**

Flipping involves taking the negative value of a question or statement and discovering the positive that is hidden within it.

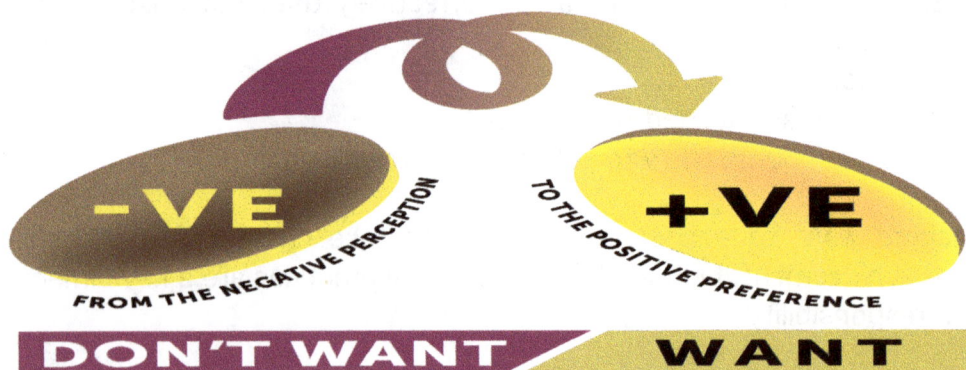

-VE
FROM THE NEGATIVE PERCEPTION

+VE
TO THE POSITIVE PREFERENCE

**DON'T WANT**      **WANT**

---

[3] 'Flipping', as taught to me by Judy Hatswell, a Senior Faculty member of Glasser Australia, is a descriptive way of reframing a negative perception to a positive preference.

The key step is to notice that every negative is a 'don't want', which is the polar opposite of a want.

If a student 'does not want' to do something, then there is something that they would prefer to do instead. When students 'don't want' to attempt something difficult, because they fear failure, what they do want is to be successful.

When a young person tells us that they feel limited by the options we offer ('I don't want to do any of those things') then they either want more freedom of choice or they are thinking about what they would prefer to do.

Any time that a student tells us that they are bored, or tell you: 'This is a waste of time', it's because they would prefer to do something that they believe would be more meaningful or enjoyable.

Flipping enables us to go beyond the negative to discover the positive want. The only thing we can do with a negative perception is acknowledge it (which is important because we want the student to know we are listening to them) and then use intuition combined with experience to speculate or **guess** what the opposite is.

The table below can help your intuition. A negative perception is never need-satisfying, so the table is organised around the five needs. On the left is language that will point to an unsatisfied need. On the right are the feelings and thoughts connected with need-satisfaction.

| Negative perception | Positive value |
| --- | --- |
| Lonely, left out, disconnected, unwanted, isolated, alone, ignored | Connected, involved, included, cared about, considered, liked, loved, befriended |
| Helpless, not respected, fragile, frustrated, ignored, unsure, not capable, unsuccessful, incompetent, unsure, uncertain, unvalued | Confident composed, capable, respected, valued, competent, able, successful, important, thriving, effective, skilled |
| Frustrated, constrained, limited, coerced, forced, obstructed, restricted, reliant | Free, autonomous, independent, self—sufficient, in control |
| Bored, tired of, weary of, uninterested, dull, tedious, | Learning, enjoying, stimulated, interested, entertained, challenged, having fun, |
| Fearful, threatened, frightened, apprehensive, intimidated, bullied, alarmed, insecure, pessimistic | Safe, secure, confident, protected, trusting, well, optimistic, hopeful, self-assured, calm, brave |

**For example**, a student might say: 'This is boring'. Instead of feeling criticised, you can respond with: 'I am sorry that you don't find this interesting' (acknowledging their perception). 'Will it make a difference if you know how useful this will be to you when you have understood or succeeded with it?'

Similarly, if a young person tells you: 'I will never be able to do this work!', you can respond with: 'I can see that you are feeling stuck at the moment.' (acknowledge the feeling). 'However, if you were confident of success, would you be prepared to keep trying until it makes sense?'

Notice that the 'want' at the end of each example is always presented as a question. If the student has a different want, they will usually accept the invitation to tell you what it is.

In a situation where you might feel criticised by a comment such as: 'You are being so unfair to me!', a helpful response could be: 'You think that I am treating you differently? If you understood that I am paying special attention to you because I want you to do well, would that make things better for both of us?'

**A couple of tips:**

1. One of the main challenges of the FLIP is that the language of the negative perception is sometimes ambiguous, so you often have to 'guess' at the underlying value. However, it does not matter if you get it wrong – your attempts to understand what the other person wants will sound positive to them.

2. Remember to acknowledge the young person's concern. There will be an emotion in the negative perception. Use empathic listening (2nd Perceptual Position - see Section 12.3) to recognise and acknowledge the emotion and the concern. When you paraphrase the concern in this way it often makes it easier to find the FLIP!

3. The FLIP is the first part of the invitation to responsibility. If the person whom you are talking with resists taking responsibility, they will keep **flipping back** to the negative perception. Be sanguine about this. Just flip again (and, if required again and again). You can't force anyone to accept responsibility for pursuing what they say that they want. What **you** can do is refuse to accept responsibility for their negative complaints. Never give up. Keep flipping!

## 5.7
## ☑ ADOPT

### MAINTAIN STUDENTS' ATTENTION WITH QUALITY TEACHING PRACTICES

It's stating the obvious to observe that if our teaching is dull, and what we are teaching is irrelevant or inaccessible to the students, then it is less likely that students will be engaged and behave responsibly. What teachers do, and how they do it, matters.[4]

I have often shown beginning teachers the 'Economics Teacher section' from the film: 'Ferris Buehler's Day Out'. In this film clip, the teacher continually asks for student input ("Anyone? Anyone?") but clearly does not want it or need it. The lesson is essentially a monologue and the students are passive observers. In this environment, students are unlikely to manage themselves well because the teacher is not regulating their own behaviours in ways that will engage the students.

The opposite of Ferris Buehler's teacher is what I describe as the 6Q teacher. If the students become disruptive, despite being taught how to self-manage, you might use the Quality Teaching checklist below to work out what is going wrong.

## 6 Dimensions of Quality Teaching:

**Q1 Interactive.** Whatever instructional method is used it should be interactive enough for students to be able to participate. Learning is not a spectator activity! Even adult learners disengage when they are not active participants in the teaching and learning process.

**Q2 Inclusive.** Everything that is taught must be accessible to all the students in the class. The test is always: 'Can what I am teaching be **used** in some way by every student in the class?' Everything that is taught doesn't need to be accessible but it must be inclusive enough to engage all students. Often this will require sufficient

---

[4] Many years ago, a teacher told me: "What I teach is often boring and irrelevant to the students." When I asked: "Why are you teaching boring and meaningless work?" his reply was: "Because it is in the curriculum"! What this teacher did not grasp is the irrevocable connection between teaching and learning. 'Covering the curriculum' is pointless if student learning is not the outcome!

differentiation of the content and processes to give everyone a chance of understanding what is taught and achieving their **personal best**.

**Q3 Interesting**. One of my colleagues often shares her belief that 'you have to be interested to be interesting'. As teachers, our degree of interest in and curiosity about the subject matter or skills we are presenting often shines through our teaching. We can be sure that if we are teaching material that is not interesting to us, it will not be interesting to our students either.

**Q4 Instructionally appropriate.** The instructional practices used need to be tailored to the current ability of the students to self-manage. It would be inadvisable to ask a class whose self-managing skills are only just emerging to engage in long periods of independent learning. As we choose from the smorgasbord of instructional strategies presented in the table below, the best practice would be to choose a mode of instruction that is suitable for the level of self-management usually demonstrated by the class (or one step more responsible in order to stretch their self-management capability), but not to expect responsible autonomy too soon.

| Lecture | Demonstration | Guided Practice |
|---|---|---|
| Independent Practice | Tutorial | Group Discovery |
| Independent Research | Skill Practices | Discussion |
| Collaborative Learning | Seminar | Problem-solving |

**Q5 Includes informative** feedback for students as they demonstrate their capabilities. The NLP dictum: 'There is no failure, only feedback' only applies if the feedback supports the next stage of learning. All feedback should *feedforward*[5] to a new task or learning episode. The more *feedforward* the teacher provides, the more likely the students are to keep achieving personal best in everything they attempt. (Read more about this in Section 9)

---

[5] *Feedforward is a term originated by Rob Stones and Judy Hatswell. (See Section 9 for more information.)*

**Q6** **Intelligible criteria** for success. Often the difference between the relative success of two students comes down to the difference in their understanding of how to be successful. When the criteria for success are clearly presented in age-appropriate and student-friendly language, every student has a chance of success.

## THE COLLABORATIVE CLASSROOM & SELF-MANAGEMENT

It is not possible to separate student self-management from the creation of a collaborative classroom culture. Passivity is not characteristic of a young person who is taking responsibility for their learning and achievement.

The more a student sees themselves as an active contributor to culture and learning in the classroom, the more likely it is that they will regard self-management as completely natural.

### 6.1

## ☑ ADOPT

### THE CREATION OF A NEED-SATISFYING CLASSROOM

As you will read in Section 8, every person has genetic needs, and our intrinsic motivation revolves around satisfying these needs.

As teachers, it can't be our job to satisfy the students' needs. We can't satisfy their needs for them. Because every student is internally controlled, they are the only ones who can find ways to satisfy their needs.

Our job as teachers is to create a classroom culture that enables them to find collaborative and responsible ways to satisfy their need to be:
- Safe.
- Competent and respected.
- Autonomous within classroom boundaries.
- Cared about within a supportive relationship with their teacher and classmates.
- Learning with enjoyment.

If students are able to satisfy their needs responsibly, they are likely to manage themselves in a way that supports classroom effectiveness. If we look at the flip side of this, it's easy to see that the students who are disruptive in the classroom are those who:
- Feel threatened or uncertain about what is happening in the classroom.
- Are not achieving, or feel they are not respected.
- Perceive that they are unwilling participants in learning activities.
- Are not getting on well with the teacher or their classmates.
- Find the learning unenjoyable or boring.

The challenge for teachers is to create a classroom environment full of opportunities for every student to satisfy their needs. Some questions we can ask ourselves are:
- Does every student feel safe from criticism or bullying?
- Are the classroom routines so well established that there is a sense of certainty in the class?
- Do all the students know how to do the work that is expected of them?
- Is there an opportunity for every student to make progress in their learning?
- Do all the students have the pre-requisite skills to do the work expected of them?
- Has the usefulness or relevance of the work been explained to the students?
- Do the students know how to delay gratification well enough to persist with the work set?
- Are students given enough choices in how they do the work to feel autonomous?
- Has the work and assessment been adapted enough to make it accessible to each student?
- Do the students in the classroom enjoy supportive relationships with each other and with the teacher?
- Is the classroom a joyful place?

If we answer no to these and similar questions, then we can take the opportunity to work with the students using one of the strategies in this section.

## 6.2

☑ **ADOPT**

### CONNECTING BEHAVIOURS

Adopt and be the champion of behaviours that will build even more positive relationships with all your students **and** between student and student.

When students believe that you care about them, that you respect them and that you are genuinely doing your best to contribute to their wellbeing, they will trust you.

That trust means that even when you are teaching something that they find challenging they will do their best because they know that you will not waste their time or teach them something that they are incapable of understanding.

Similarly, when students understand that specific connecting behaviours create a good relationship between them, and that other behaviours damage the relationships, they have clear shared guidelines for how to treat each other. Many of these may have been included in the 'boundaries' that you established, but it is worth spending time on the connecting and disconnecting behaviours.

Ensure that your reasons for wanting to strengthen the relationships with them are no mystery! Teach the students that there are connecting and disconnecting behaviours, and the effects of using these.

Most students already know that there are behaviours that help them to get on well with each other and that will improve their relationship with you. You can use their knowledge and experience to come up with a list that puts this in their own words. You can use the list above to help you. However, I suggest that you encourage the students to come up with their own list and present these ideas in language that makes sense to them.

Having a clear list of behaviours that will support positive relationships helps you to begin to teach them the habit of self-evaluation. When a student is criticising

**Connecting behaviours**

- Caring
- Listening
- Liking
- Supporting
- Contributing
- Encouraging
- Trusting
- Befriending
- Negotiating
- Respecting Differences

another member of the class, or making a disparaging comment, or using bullying behaviours, you can ask:

- o Will that behaviour improve relationships in this classroom, or make them worse?
- o Is that a connecting behaviour or a disconnecting one?

The more that you ask students to self-evaluate their behaviour, the more likely it is that they will ask themselves these same questions. This is far more powerful and effective than reprimanding or correcting students. Remember that questions tend to activate the brain's control centre. This means that the students' knowledge about which behaviours connect and which disconnect becomes associated with specific behaviours.

## 6.3
## ☒ AVOID

### DISCONNECTING BEHAVIOURS

Avoid the use of disconnecting behaviours in your own communication practices.  It is as important to establish behaviours that should be evaded as it is to work on the connecting behaviours.

In particular, work hard to eliminate these behaviours from your repertoire:

- * Punishments
- * Threats
- * Rewards*see below.

All these disconnecting behaviours are experienced as coercive. When you use them, they imply that you have (and will use) superior power over the students. Young people will take seriously your intention for them to become self-managing if you manage yourself well in this regard.

*Disconnecting Behaviours*

- Ignoring
- Criticising
- Blaming
- Controlling
- Complaining
- Nagging
- Threatening
- Punishing
- Guilting
- Rewarding to Control

When things go wrong – as when a student manages themselves badly - it is especially important to avoid disconnecting behaviours and to replace them with the various 'work-it-out' strategies presented in later sections of this book.

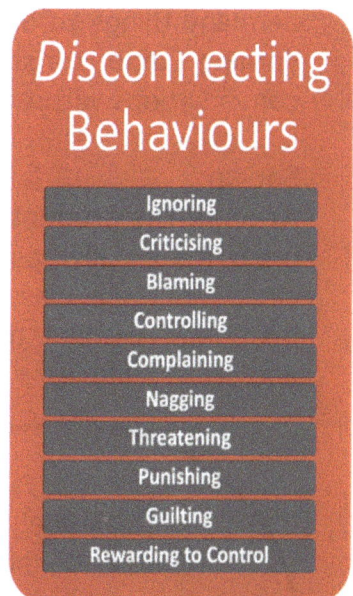

Ask students to identify disconnecting behaviours - behaviours that make things worse in the classroom (and at home) - and be open and honest about your intention to eliminate these behaviours from your own repertoire.

* If you have not yet read the sections on rewards, and you are thinking of rewards as helpful and harmless, you may be surprised to see them identified as 'disconnecting'. Please reserve judgment until you have read the explanations in the next section on 'delaying gratification'.

## 6.4

## ☑ ADOPT

### USE CLASS MEETINGS

As you make the changes from teacher control to student self-control, there will be many things to discuss with the class. Conducting a **Classroom Meeting** or a **Yarning Circle** is a strategy that you can adopt for these open, but structured, conversations with the class.

**Set-up.**
**Arrange the students in a circle,** with the teacher sitting in the circle with the class. It's usually best to take the class outside to a space that is suitable for a circle. Once the 'class meeting' has become a familiar process, you can hold quick 'meetings' without moving into a circle, but it's always best to introduce the activity in a circle.

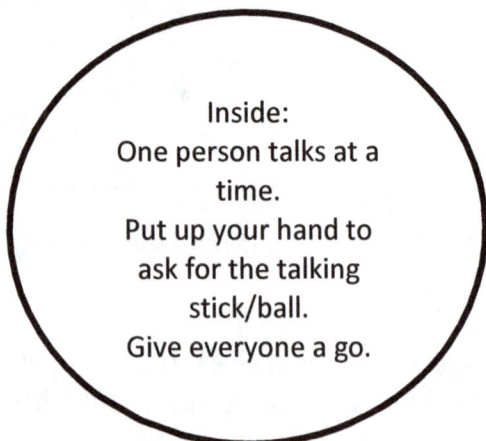

Inside:
One person talks at a time.
Put up your hand to ask for the talking stick/ball.
Give everyone a go.

**Establish the boundaries** for this activity:
There is usually no need to elaborate on what is 'outside' the circle, unless you feel that the class needs that additional structure.

**The topic for the discussion** can either be related to something that the class needs to agree upon, or to introduce something in the curriculum and find out what students already know.

Holding a class meeting demonstrates your willingness, as a teacher, to listen to the ideas of the class whilst you participate as an 'equal' voice.

A **Class Meeting** has a defined structure as explained below. A **Yarning Circle** may have a looser structure and can be used to help the students deliberately practise connecting behaviours, improve their listening skills and enhance the quality of their relationships.

## 6.4
## THE CLASSROOM MEETING.

**The 3 steps** of a classroom meeting are: DEFINE. PERSONALISE. CHALLENGE. This is not a rigid structure, but a way of systematically taking the conversation to deeper levels.

**Example: a classroom meeting about 'self-management'.**

**Step 1: DEFINE** self-control. Ask the question: "What does Self-Management mean?"

**Step 2: PERSONALISE** the definition by asking students what it would mean for them and the class if everyone improved their communication habits, and everyone (including the teacher) took responsibility for managing themselves well.

**Step 3: CHALLENGE** the students to think and talk about the difficulties of establishing the expectation that 'every student is responsible for behaving well' and that the teacher's job is not to correct them but to ask them: "Is that behaviour responsible?"

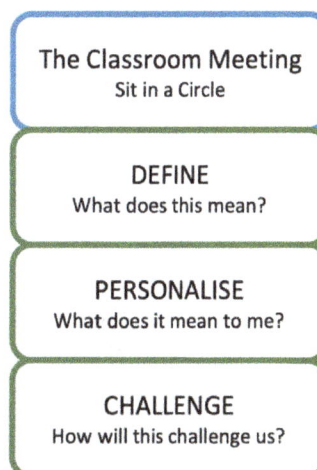

> **The Classroom Meeting**
> Sit in a Circle
>
> **DEFINE**
> What does this mean?
>
> **PERSONALISE**
> What does it mean to me?
>
> **CHALLENGE**
> How will this challenge us?

The teacher might expect some sceptical questions during this class meeting. Questions such as: "Will you stop telling us what to do?" It's best to be honest with your answer. Explain that there are times when you **will** need to give instructions, That's part of your job. However, also explain that you as the teacher will be learning to change from depending upon controlling instructions to teaching them how to self-manage. This is your goal. It will require quite a few changes in behaviour from both teacher and student.

Also explain that **as the teacher,** your job is to teach. You will have to give lots of instructions as an expert. You will often have to direct the content of the lessons, choose the most effective strategies for learning, and the best processes to use with the class.

Expecting students to self-manage will not interfere with the job of the teacher. Teachers have to instruct, conduct lessons, explain, tutor, give information, guide, and demonstrate.

What you will do is focus on all the behaviours connected to the job of teaching. What the teacher and the class will learn together is how to successfully make the transition that is needed for student behaviour to become the job of the student.

## 6.5

## ☑ ADOPT

### USE YARNING CIRCLES

### The Yarning Circle [1, 2]

The Yarning Circle draws on the cultural practices of the First Nations people of Australia. A Yarning Circle is a harmonious, creative, and collaborative way of communicating in a group to:

- Encourage responsible, respectful, and honest interactions, and establish trusting relationships.
- Support participants to be 'present in the moment' and listen intently.
- Foster accountability while providing a safe place to hear and be heard.
- Acknowledge the strengths and opinions of other participants and to make a contribution in return.

---

[1] QCAA. (2020, October 25). *Yarning circles.* (Q. Government, Producer) Retrieved February 2021, from Queensland Curriculum and Assessment Authority:

[2] Miller, A. (2020, October 22). Everton Park State School Framework for Wellbeing. Brisbane, QLD, Australia.

A Yarning Circle is usually initiated or hosted by an individual — a teacher, a student, or a visitor. Yarning Circles can take several formats, but the following guidelines generally apply:

1. **The host** explains the purpose of the Circle and reminds the students of the historical and cultural significance of this practice.
2. **The host uses focus questions.** Yarning Circles can be undertaken for many reasons. The host introduces the purpose of the Yarning Circle or the focus question to participants.
3. **Everyone sits in a circle** where they can see each other and hear each other. Participants are encouraged to listen thoughtfully to the views of others. Everyone is considered equal within the Circle, and no voice is of greater importance than another.

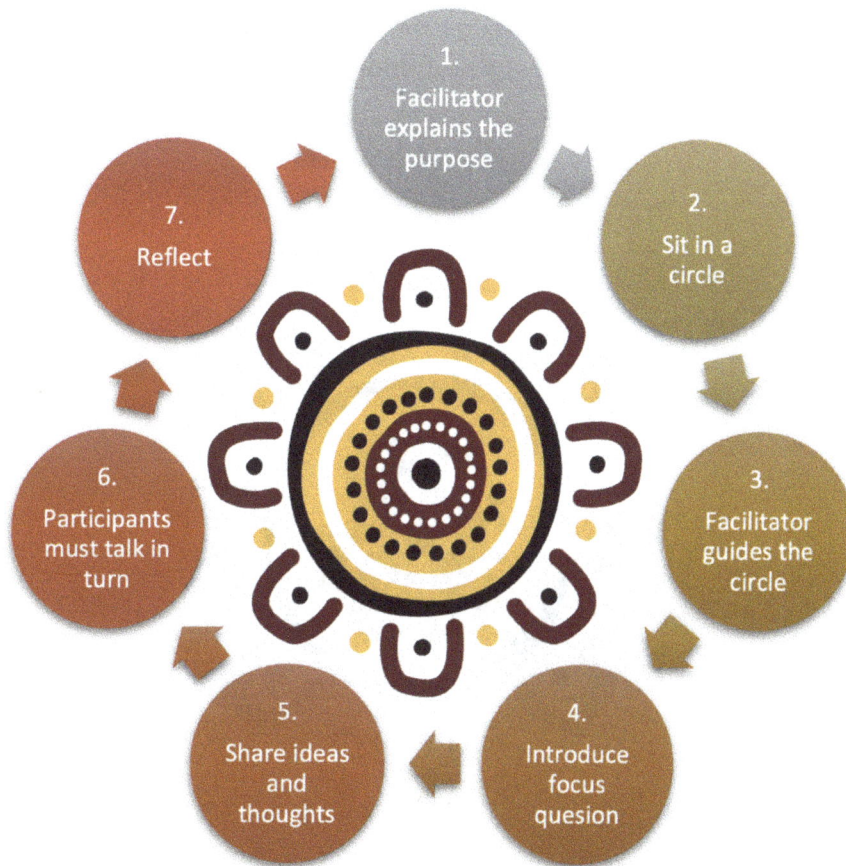

4. **The host guides the Circle.** They take the facilitator's role in supporting students to communicate respectfully and share their own stories without

interruption. The facilitator is equal to the students, so they should also share within the group.

5. **Everyone is encouraged to share ideas and thoughts.** The facilitator encourages participants to take turns to talk and to promote reciprocal sharing and learning. Time can be allocated for participants to write or draw their thoughts after each person speaks. The host can provide butcher's paper in the middle of the circle for participants to record their thoughts or hold the Circle outside of the classroom so that participants can draw their thoughts in the earth. Each participant speaks from their strengths, and everyone listens to the speaker. Sometimes participants may wish to pass their turn.

6. **Participants must talk in turn.** To question others, a participant's turn must come around again. This encourages participants to listen attentively to the other participants.

7. **The Circle is an opportunity to reflect.** Sometimes, there is no need for a follow-up. At other times, issues may be identified that require actions. If so, these actions must be agreed upon in the Circle or followed up in future Yarning Circles.

# ~ SECTION 7 ~

## DELAYING GRATIFICATION

### 7.1
☑ **ADOPT**

#### TEACH STUDENTS HOW TO DELAY GRATIFICATION

Learning to delay gratification is the capability that every young person needs to acquire if they are to flourish and become responsible and resilient.

Schools often do not teach it deliberately, and yet many of their student management issues come directly from students who have not learned to delay gratification. This is not just an issue for Primary Schools. Many teenagers do not know how to manage their impulsivity. Their inability to delay gratification can be the origin of many of the difficulties that they have with schooling.

**Delaying gratification is the ability to defer immediate satisfaction in exchange for a long-term gain.**

Learning to delay gratification is of critical importance for leading a successful life. If you are a teacher, you will have acquired this ability. You could not have completed the study and training required of a professional without it. Yet every one of us needs to call on this ability in our daily life, and we all benefit from practising it as a discipline almost every day.

The brain is naturally impulsive. Without learning, it tends to reach out for what it wants without delay. It is the mind, our conscious awareness, that enables us to wait and work towards long-term benefits. Because the mind can project our thoughts forward and backward in time, it can anticipate the greater reward that will come with persistence and sustained effort.

What we observe in younger children is that they often have not acquired this ability. When they want something, they want it 'now'! That's the natural preference of the brain. Children must learn to delay gratification. Impulsiveness is natural. Deferring pleasure until later is not.

Fortunately, by the time that they come to school, most children have learned to delay gratification to some extent through the modelling of their family. Sadly, some young people do not have the benefit of this parental modelling. If they do not subsequently learn to defer satisfaction at school they may never learn it. Without this ability, many people lead difficult lives. They are over-represented in prisons and amongst the disadvantaged in our society. For some, the school classroom may be their last chance to acquire this vital life skill.

As teachers, one of the most important things that we can teach is this ability to wait; to put off any immediate pleasure in order to be intrinsically rewarded at a later time.

Promoting this capability with students is not easy. This section offers some examples of strategies that will help young people learn how to delay gratification. Because setting future goals is central to delaying gratification, the strategies in Section 14 on Goal-setting can also be used.


## 7.2
## ☑ ADOPT

SET GOALS - FOR BOTH INDIVIDUAL STUDENTS AND THE CLASS.

Setting goals that require working towards an achievement is one of the most effective ways of teaching delay of gratification. For the students who are already familiar with putting off the reward until later, setting goals is familiar, but is always something that can be improved. Students who are still learning delay of gratification can benefit greatly from setting small goals and achieving them. With a whole class, you can construct a workflow process that helps students to understand how to work towards a goal or purpose by illustrating the process:

- Our specific goal (or learning intention) is ….

- We will achieve this by ....
- The steps to achieving our purpose are ....
- Things that will help us reach our goal are ....
- We will know we have reached our goal when....

Teachers who are accustomed to beginning each lesson by making the learning intentions explicit can easily expand on that by adding the kind of workflow process shown above.

Our problem as teachers is that although we know that there are steps to achieving our lesson intentions, we don't always make them explicit. The students who have been previously shown this step-by-step approach to achieving a goal will see this process in action. Young people who have not yet learned this will need it explained. Displaying or explaining the process we are following will help students who haven't yet acquired the same level of familiarity with the process.

**Delaying gratification is much easier for students who have confidence that following a one-stage-at-a-time process will lead to success.**

## 7.3
## ☑ ADOPT

### GIVE FEEDBACK THAT ATTRIBUTES SUCCESS TO PATIENT EFFORT

Most teachers are aware of Carol Dweck's work on the importance of a 'Growth Mindset'.[1] The crux of her research is on the development of positive attitudes to self, and the importance of adopting the belief that ability is developed rather than fixed. However, it is also important to notice how the strategies that she suggests enhance the ability to work patiently towards a goal.

Giving feedback that draws attention to the way that persistence and determination contribute to a student's progress towards a goal is always helpful. When the teacher comments on the patience shown by the student, and the way that they have taken the time to produce quality work instead of rushing, this contributes to the ability to delay gratification.

---

[1] Carol Dweck: 'Mindset- The New Psychology of Success', Ballantine 2007

Sometimes, teachers of High School age students come to believe that strategies like these are important for their primary education colleagues, and therefore ignore their relevance for older students. However, the teenage years are when an inability to delay gratification starts to bite. Tasks and expectations become even more complex and require the ability to persist, to work through a process, and to learn from mistakes.

One of the qualities I have most admired in my teacher colleagues has been their ability to break a complex task into small chunks for the students who are easily overwhelmed. Setting achievable milestones within a task, drawing the students' attention to their own progress and gradually developing their capacity for persistence have been shown to be both achievable and rewarding.

## 7.4

## ☒ AVOID

### REWARDS THAT FEED THE HABIT OF INSTANT GRATIFICATION![2]

It's a great temptation for a teacher to give students gold stars, stickers, or merit certificates to encourage or reward them. Many teachers tell me it feels harmless (or even helpful) to give these interim rewards as short-term motivation.

Unfortunately, there are two kinds of problem with this kind of instant reward for short-term effort:
- It interferes with the ability to learn delayed gratification, especially when used frequently. When students get used to the idea that they will get a short-term reward for minimal effort, they do not develop the habit of persistence - a habit that is essential for delaying gratification.

---

[2] For alternatives to rewards, see the section on genetic needs in Section 2, and Section 13 on setting goals.

Teachers often provide these short-term incentives with the best of intentions, not realising how easily students (and their parents!) become habituated to constant rewarding, instead of working towards longer-term achievements.[3] This is often even more of a concern when teachers over-reward students who present with problem behaviours, not realising that they are encouraging their lack of self-control by using rewards to control them.

- Accumulating external rewards also interferes with a student's capacity to develop an internal locus of control. One of the long-term sources of resilience is the ability to originate our motivation from inside ourselves. The alternative is to develop an external locus of control and **become a person who only knows that they are doing well when someone tells them so**. Having an **internal** locus of control enables us to be self-reliant. Needing external validation leaves us helpless victims of the opinions of other people.

You will have noticed that this book stresses the importance of self-evaluation: the ability of a student to evaluate and control their behaviours. Self-evaluation is an essential competence for children as they learn to manage themselves, and it enables them to acquire the internal locus of control that is important for self-management.

## 7.5
## ☑ ADOPT

**Any of these 10 additional strategies that help students to develop an internal locus of control and delay gratification:**

I.   Teacher modelling. As mentioned before, students learn more from who we are than from what we know. Dr William Glasser, in his work with delinquent teenagers, built 'never give up' into the procedures that he used to teach them to take control of their own lives.

---

[3] Refer to Alfie Kohn: 'Punished by Rewards', and the material in the section on rewarding to control.

'Never give up' is a mantra I have seen used by many of the great teachers I have worked alongside or talked with. Telling your students, quite explicitly: "I will never give up on you. You are a 'work-in-progress," and "I will be here to help you and teach you until you are happily taking control of yourself'" is both reassuring and inspiring for a young person whose self-esteem is low.

When they observe that you mean what you say, and that every time they test your resolve by behaving badly or giving up, you are there, ready to begin again, they begin to understand the nature of resilient determination.

II.	Maze planning. Use simple mazes with the goal in the centre as a fun introduction to planning. The goal that students are working towards is the treasure in the centre. The treasure can be solving a problem, a piece of writing, making a papier mâché castle or anything that has a product. The pathways through the maze can be labelled with anything that has to be done to achieve the goal.

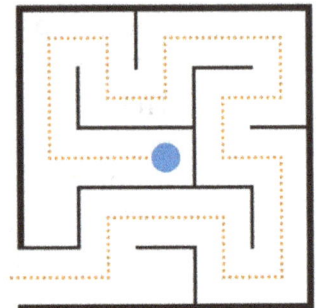

III.	Similarly, teach **prioritisation** by embedding it into the way in which you teach students to plan and sequence longer-term tasks. This can be taught to students when they are very young - but it's very important for students of all ages. When we teach our students that every extended task or assignment can be broken into a sequence of 'X first, then Y, and only after that do Z', they learn to trust the process of assembling a task or assignment in sequence.

IV.	Read stories to younger children that emphasise patience and taking turns, such as 'Patient Ninja', and 'Croc needs to wait'. There are many such stories that will appeal to younger children and provide an opportunity for discussion about the theme of delaying gratification.

V.	Similarly, younger children can play games that involve taking turns. There are many such games in the 'Play is the Way' curriculum for Early Years schooling. 'Stop and Go' games are suitable for younger students. They enable the teacher to emphasise the importance of **waiting** as a step towards success. Even students of secondary school age (and adults) benefit from playing games that the teacher can use to demonstrate and practise turn-taking and the need to use patient routines and systems in the way they work together.

'Follow Ball', 'GO', and 'Improving the Product' all involve such sequencing.[4] The turn-taking procedures in Class Meetings and 'Yarning Circles' are other examples of activities that help students 'wait their turn' and, of course, all team-related activities need these skills for their effectiveness.

VI. Use **'if-then'** to encourage students to associate their self-control with good events. When students ask to do something they like doing, but the time is not right, avoid saying 'not now' and substitute **'if-then',** as in: **If** we all finish our writing task before morning break, **then** we can play 'The Jedi Mind game'.

VII. When looking forward to an event that is coming up for the class or school, mark off the days on the calendar as the countdown for the event. The more that the students can be involved in and contribute to the event, the better. If appropriate, use the language of long-term thinking and goal-setting. For example: 'We now have ten days before our parent morning tea. What do we have to do to prepare for the event?' ('Who is going to do what?', and 'When will it need to be completed?').

VIII. Use **timelines** wherever possible in planning. Students with some personality types (those with a preference for making decisions) quite naturally think of time as running a line between the past and the future. Those with a preference for the present moment don't organise time in their heads in the same way. For these students creating timelines for planning helps them to be organised and to associate the intrinsic reward of task completion with the prior activity and with the preparation that goes on before the task is completed successfully.

IX. Calm the impulse. If you are using whole class instruction and calling on students to respond one at a time, students will often have to manage the long gaps between opportunities to offer their ideas or provide the answer to your questions.
   - These occasions are an opportunity to teach self-calming activities that will be useful in all sorts of situations where **waiting** is needed.
   - Teaching students how to belly-breathe or to use progressive muscle relaxation helps them with self-control.

---

[4] Rob Stones: 'The Tao of Team in Practice', FutureShape Publishing 2020.

- I used to demonstrate isometric strength exercises like pushing against your hands or pulling against them, to give students something useful to do while they are waiting their turn.
- Teachers often discourage doodling, but it is a good way for students to occupy themselves while they are waiting. If students have to wait for your attention, they can use positive doodles to frame the question they want to ask you or work out why they are stuck.
- With those young people who 'know the answer' and find it hard to resist calling out what they know, I used to teach them to write down their answers and then tick them off when they are correct. They would experience deferred satisfaction by showing me all of the ticks later.
- Allow students who have particular difficulty with impulse control to bring and use a stress ball as a self-calming practice.

X.  Teach one of the many 'steps to a solution' problem-solving practices to the students. There are many of these, but the simplest is probably:
- State the problem.
- What will you be able to do if this problem is solved?
- What choices do you have?
- Implement one of your choices.
- Evaluate the result.

All step-by-step processes help students to understand the link between a patiently implemented process and the eventual satisfying result.

# ~ SECTION 8 ~

## ☑ ADOPT

### TEACH STUDENTS HOW THE BRAIN WORKS

When students learn how their brains work, their capacity to manage their thoughts, actions, and feelings improves significantly. Specifically, the ability of students to self-manage is supported by:

**1. Knowing that they have genetic needs.**
- Discovering that we all have choices about how to satisfy those needs.
- Realising that we feel happiest when our needs are satisfied.
- Referring to the needs and discussing the various ways to gratify the needs, either responsibly or thoughtlessly, brings an informed maturity to the way that students think about their behaviour and motivation, as well as the way in which these needs affect other people.

**2. Exploring the four elements of behaviour through the 'Behaviour Car'.** This helps students to appreciate the interplay of their thoughts and emotions, body states and actions. With this understanding, they can more easily take control of their total behaviour and will acquire a public language to discuss the complexities of their thoughts, actions and feelings.

**3. Identifying the mechanism of their motivation.** Knowing how motivation works expands the opportunities for choice. Through understanding why they do what they do, students become better placed to manage themselves. Understanding motivation requires knowing about three key elements of their mental life:

I. The people, ideas, and experiences in their own Quality World.

II. The uniqueness of their perceptual system.

III. The way that motivation comes from comparing the 'wants' in the Quality World with their perception of current circumstances. Teaching these dimensions of how the brain works can begin in Year One and subsequently be taught in an age-appropriate way to school students of every age.[1]

---

[1] Ivan Honey's 'Get Happier Schools' project introduces the brain and behaviour to young students through Doug Dragster and his Adventures. It's an imaginative way to teach students how to understand and regulate their behaviour.

## 8.1

☑ **ADOPT**

### TEACH THE NEEDS

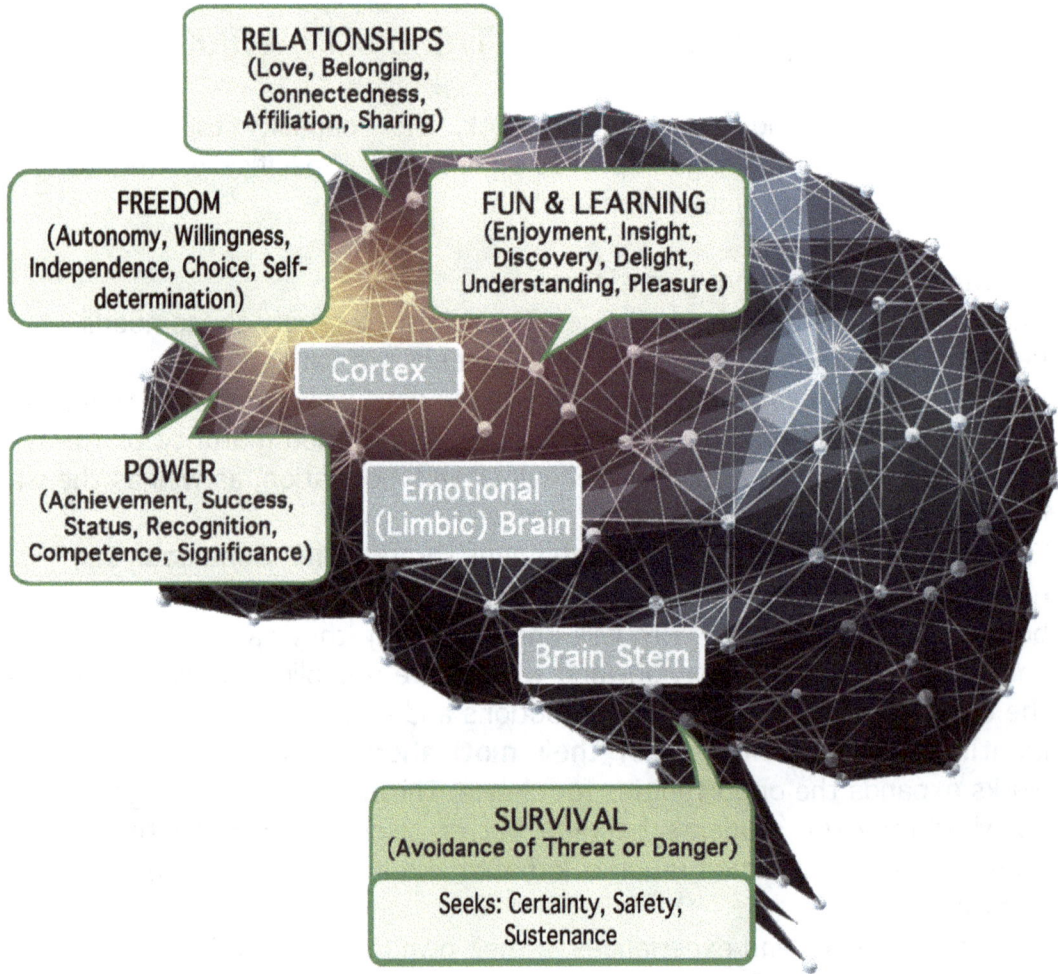

**RELATIONSHIPS**
(Love, Belonging, Connectedness, Affiliation, Sharing)

**FREEDOM**
(Autonomy, Willingness, Independence, Choice, Self-determination)

**FUN & LEARNING**
(Enjoyment, Insight, Discovery, Delight, Understanding, Pleasure)

Cortex

**POWER**
(Achievement, Success, Status, Recognition, Competence, Significance)

Emotional (Limbic) Brain

Brain Stem

**SURVIVAL**
(Avoidance of Threat or Danger)

Seeks: Certainty, Safety, Sustenance

Teach the students about the five human NEEDS. Explain that we all have genetic needs for:

**Relationships:** Love, belonging, connectedness, friends.
**Power:** Achievement, competence, success.
**Autonomy:** Freedom, willingness, independence.
**Fun and Learning:** Enjoyment, insight, discovery.
**Survival:** Safety, certainty, sustenance.

Everyone thrives when their needs are met. They feel happy and in control when they:

1. Have a sense of achievement or feel in control.
2. Are enjoying good relationships with others – feeling respected and appreciated.
3. Have sufficient freedom to make at least some choices and feel that they are doing things willingly.
4. Learn and have fun.
5. Feel safe when things are predictable.

When teaching the 'needs' there is plenty of opportunity for discussion about the different ways young people can satisfy their own needs:

- Share some examples of how each of the needs can be met. It is sometimes fun to speculate about how famous people or cartoon characters seem to get their needs met, and then to talk about how class members satisfy their own needs.
- Conduct discussions with the students about ways in which their needs can be met, either responsibly or selfishly. A Class Meeting or a Yarning Circle provide good opportunities for these discussions.

**Make sure students know how to satisfy their needs responsibly**. This is crucial! Students can't be expected to choose responsible behaviours if they don't know how! For example, if a student does not have the social skills to relate well to their classmates or adults, then they have to be taught these skills before they can be expected to use them. If a student is not able to meet their need for power and achievement through classroom success, then they will inevitably attempt to find other ways to meet this need by establishing their significance or status in ways that are not conducive to learning.

It can be fun to conduct some demonstrations and role plays to illustrate the difference between learning-friendly ways of meeting student needs and ways that are not appropriate. Activities such as these build a repertoire of language and behaviours that encourage the needs to be discussed freely.

# ☑ ADOPT

## THE CAR METAPHOR

Teach the students about the four elements of behaviour using the 'car' metaphor. Just as the car has 4 wheels, behaviour has 4 elements: Acting, Thinking, Feeling and Physiology.

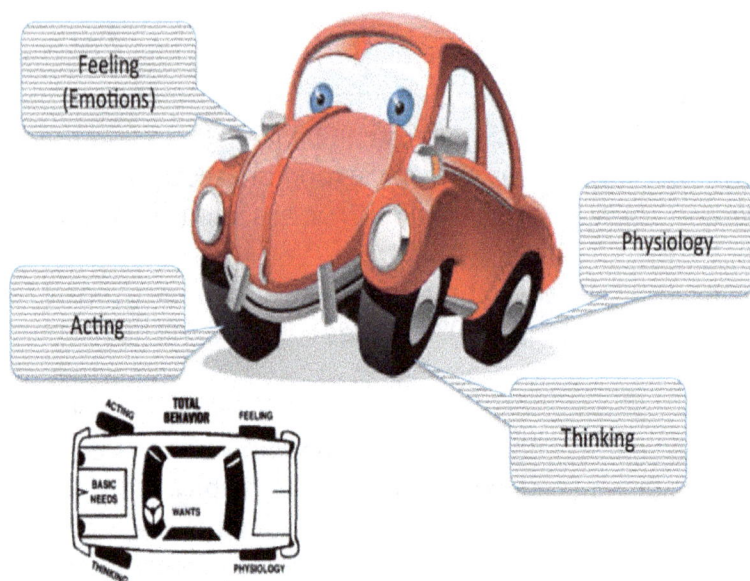

Students generally do not have a language with which to talk about the specific features of self-management.

Generalised instructions such as 'behave yourself' or 'control yourself' are no help, because they are neither specific nor informative.

The car metaphor provides students with language and a visual concept that makes it possible to discuss specific behaviours and to talk and think about what to do to self-manage.

Dr William Glasser who devised the 'behaviour car' metaphor regarded it as one of the most creative ways he had conceived for helping people to understand and control their behaviour.

When I present the behaviour car to students, I usually invite them to develop it for themselves by asking them:

1. **What are the differences between thinking and acting?**

I often encourage the comparison by asking them to perform some simple actions - and then carry out some thinking tasks. I list their responses in two columns so that we have a context for developing the car. For example:

| Thinking | Acting |
|---|---|
| Ideas | Doing |
| Reasons | Moving |
| Talking to yourself | Walking or running |
| Planning | Stretching |
| Reflecting | Performing a skill |

2. The words students come up with will be age-related, but they enable me to ask the questions:
- Which can you see, and which are invisible?
- Is an intention a thought or an action?
- What do you try to achieve with your thoughts and actions?

3. These questions invite discussion and can then be connected to the car by comparing them to the front wheels of the car. The front wheels of the car steer it so that it goes where the driver wants it to go. In the same way, the 'front wheels' of our behaviour are our best attempts to get what we want.

4. Next, I introduce the back wheels (often at a different time so that I can use 'front wheels' language with the class for a while before I introduce the back wheels). Once again, I initiate examination of these elements of behaviour with a question such as: **What are the differences between thinking and feeling?**

5. When students have identified differences between thought and feeling, I ask questions that help them understand the significance of the difference:
   o Can you control how you feel as easily as how you think?
   o When you are angry or sad, can you just tell yourself to 'cheer up'?
   o Which feelings give us energy? Which take our energy away and lead to us feeling 'down'?

6. It's then easy to teach that emotions are like our back wheels. They change the amount of energy or drive in the car, but they are not good for steering. Because emotions are our energy meter, they also let us know how we are feeling, and send us signals about whether we are in control or not.

7. Once students are talking about emotions, I introduce physiology or 'body state' by asking what is happening in our body when we are experiencing different emotions. By using examples such as excited, angry, worried,

confident, daring, and bored, I ask students to demonstrate the physiology that accompanies each different emotion.

8. From this point on, the students have enough information for me to be able to teach the remaining key concepts of the behaviour car which are:

   **A. All behaviour is TOTAL – our acting, thinking, feeling and body state are always connected. If we change one, the others change as well.**

   **B. Although we can't control our back wheels directly, they will change if we change our front wheels. Managing our thinking and acting is the key to self-control.**

   **C. Naming our behaviour, using the language of the behaviour car enables students to identify the element of behaviour that they need to focus on to manage themselves well in any situation.**

Once the car metaphor is firmly established with a class or a student, it generates very specific and helpful questions that assist students in managing their behaviour and learning. These questions might be:
- Are you on your back wheels or front wheels?
- Do you know what to do to change your back wheels?
- What kind of thinking helps you to do your best work?

You can add to their understanding by using your knowledge to explain to students why you are using 'brain breaks' or energisers, or why you set up classroom routines so that students can bring their best energy to learning.

## 8.3
## ☒ AVOID

### SAYING 'BEHAVE YOURSELF' IS MEANINGLESS

Vague phrases such as 'behave yourself' are not useful. **Everyone is always 'behaving'!** - there is always thinking, acting, feelings and a physiological state happening - so this kind of imprecise language will not help students to identify the elements of behaviour that they should focus on to improve their self-management.

Replace vague injunctions with more specific and car-related questions:

- Which wheels are you on?
- Are you on the back wheels or the front wheels?
- Do you need time (or help) to get off the back wheels?
- Which wheel will help you to move forward responsibly?

## 8.4

## ☑ ADOPT

### TEACH ABOUT PERCEPTION

Teach the students about the individual nature of perception.

This is another important piece of children's understanding of how their mind works. It is something that is best taught over time at an age-relevant level. For example: As a lesson starter, show students a colour that is between blue and green and ask them what colour it is.

Many will pick blue. Others will pick green. Explain that we all see colours differently, not because there is something different in our vision, but because of the way that we learn to give names to the visual signals that we receive.

Another way of doing this is to use an image that has some visual ambiguity, like the one illustrated.

In subsequent lessons, you can play different pieces of music, or ask children to describe tastes or smells that they like or don't like (You can give them examples.)

Always explain that our 5 senses are the way in which we take in information from outside us. Sight. Hearing. Taste. Smell. Touch. These are our windows into the world.

In all cases, make the point that the way we take in this information, and how we name it, is individual to all of us. People who see things differently from us are not necessarily wrong; they just interpret things differently.

We all 'filter' our perceptions of what is happening through our personal memories, our life and educational history, through our family and cultural values. It's no wonder that we all think differently!

Perception is something that is best taught every time an opportunity arises, and refined as children grow older. However, it is never too soon to teach perception to young people, and to take time to discuss the implications for their learning. Understanding the personal nature of perception not only helps them to understand themselves, but it is also the basis of tolerance.

## 8.5
## ☒ AVOID

### SPEAKING AS IF YOU ARE THE ORACLE!

Avoid talking with the students as if your own perceptions and opinions are certainly 'right'. Replace 'this is how things are' with 'this is how I see things.'

Talking in a way that recognises the individuality of perception enables you to explain the nature of evidence and to show how our perceptions **do change** when there is proof or grounds for an alternative belief (although of course, we are all quite capable of interpreting evidence differently!).

Learning about the individuality of perception can help students to self-manage by helping them avoid the frustration of communicating with other individuals who think differently from them.

## 8.6
☑ ADOPT

### TEACH 'THE QUALITY WORLD'

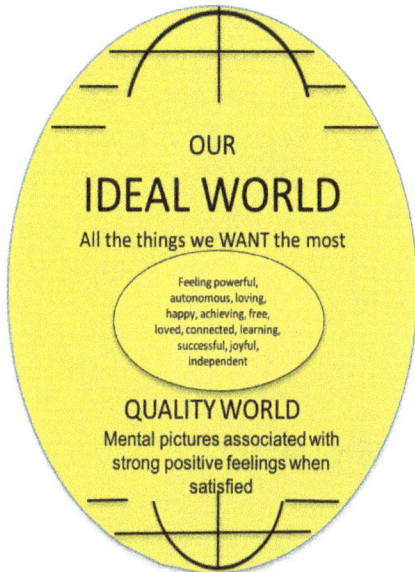

OUR

**IDEAL WORLD**

All the things we WANT the most

Feeling powerful, autonomous, loving, happy, achieving, free, loved, connected, learning, successful, joyful, independent

**QUALITY WORLD**

Mental pictures associated with strong positive feelings when satisfied

Everyone stores memories of the experiences that they have found to be need-satisfying. These are the experiences, relationships, ideas, and activities that give us pleasure. The **Quality World** or **Ideal World** is a way of describing these stores of pleasurable experiences.

The Quality World can be populated by people, places, activities, achievements, or ideas.

These distinctive experiences stand out because they are so need-satisfying. Naturally enough, we like to repeat these experiences. They are our ideal of how we would like things to be.

Teaching students about Quality is important because we want to encourage them to do Quality work – the best that they can do.

A great way to introduce them to Quality is through a meditation or reflective activity. Begin with a relaxation activity or a mindfulness exercise, and then move on to ask students to identify the people, events, activities, and achievements that are in their Quality World.

Because Quality is always need-satisfying, working from each of the needs is a good way of helping children identify the many dimensions of their Quality World. For example:
- o Who are the people whom you like to be with, who support you and whom you can rely on to help you? (Relationships and Belonging need).
- o What activities or situations bring a sense of achievement and success? (Power and Achievement need).
- o When do you feel most free? Or when do you know that you have lots of choices available to you? (Autonomy need).
- o What things do you most enjoy learning about? (Fun and Learning need).
- o At what times, or with whom, do you feel safe? (Survival need).

Explain that we all have a Quality World and that we put people, places, events, and activities in that QW when they give us pleasure.
Ask students to create a private 'map' of their own Quality World to keep in their reference folder.

Another way of thinking about our quality experiences is to realise that these are our **wants**. We have wants in every dimension of our lives, and pursuing these wants is important to the mental health of every young person. When they are actively pursuing things that they want, students tend to be energized and eager. When they don't know what they want, the tendency is to focus on the negatives: the things that they don't want.

## 8.7

## ☒ AVOID

### SOME STUDENTS HAVE VERY LITTLE IN THEIR QUALITY WORLD!

Avoid making assumptions about the Quality World that each student brings to the classroom. High-achieving, socially-skilled children will have many 'pictures' in their Quality World. Students from emotionally impoverished or traumatic backgrounds may have very little in their Quality World because they have encountered very few safe or satisfying experiences in their lives.

The challenge with these students is to overcome their natural pessimism. They don't expect success or the unconditional regard of an adult because they have rarely experienced these. The opportunity that emerges from the scarcity of their Quality experiences is that when we do make a strong connection with them, or help them to feel a sense of achievement, we have a foothold in their Quality World.

Helping students identify who and what is in their Quality World has two benefits. It helps students to understand what Quality means to them, and also helps them to actively pursue other Quality experiences. It also supports the goal of the teacher to understand their students and expose them to as much potential Quality as possible. If a student has their teacher in their Quality World, this is a great step towards a classroom culture of wellness.

At some stage after you have taught both perception and the Quality World:

## 8.8
☑ **ADOPT**

## TEACH STUDENTS HOW THEY ARE MOTIVATED

As the diagram shows, we are always comparing our ideas of what is 'Quality' or 'ideal' with what is actually happening. When there is a gap between what we think is happening and what we identify as Quality, we choose behaviours to close that gap and get more of the things that we want. This is the positive motivation to which all students have access. In the language of psychology, this is **'approach motivation'**.

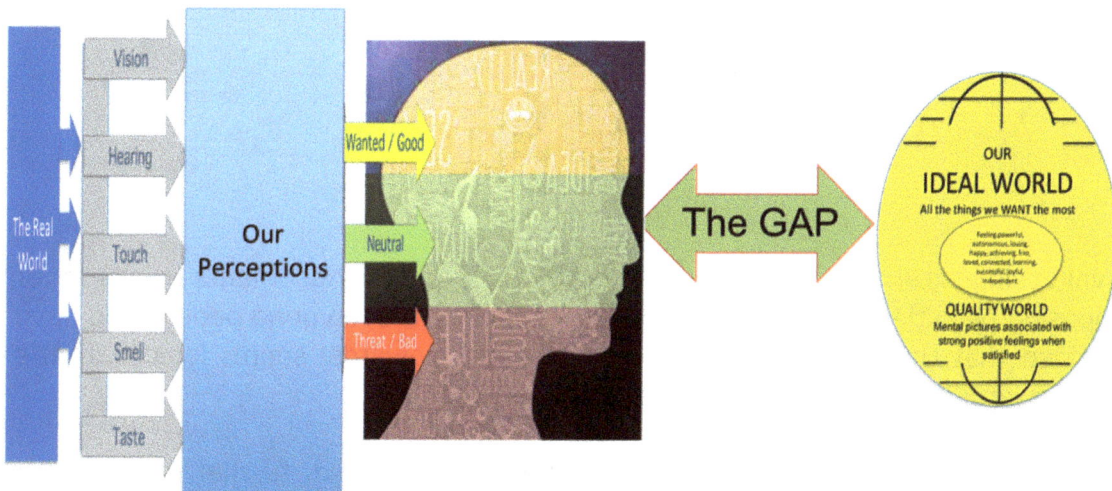

Brain-healthy activities such as goal-setting and delay of gratification depend on having positive wants to pursue. Identifying their 'wants' helps young people channel their efforts and energy into the things that will give them pleasure.

You may also explain to students that **'avoidance motivation'** or **'don't wants'** can be the alternative way in which our minds steer our behaviours. We all do avoid painful experiences or threats, but these are motivations that either STOP us from doing things or lead us to neglect opportunities: (e.g. not trying something because we fear failure).

The gap between pursuing a want and avoiding a 'don't want' is psychologically huge! Pursuing a want is energizing. It marshals the energy of young people in pursuit of quality and need-satisfaction. That is why students benefit from identifying the **wants** in their Quality World in order to give them specific goals to 'move towards', and why so much of a teacher's effectiveness resides in their ability to set achievable targets for their students, despite the wide range of ability in most classes.

When young people give up the pursuit of wants and become focused on avoiding the pain of what they don't want, there is almost always a negative change in their behaviour. Not having Quality World 'pictures' to pursue, they have no reason to 'push through' challenging activities to achieve a goal. Why should they work hard or strive to learn? Learning and achievement only make sense when there is something worthwhile to strive for.

## 8.9

## ☒ AVOID

### EXTERNAL MOTIVATION

Avoid using external motivation with students. Offering inducements (rewards) or imposing penalties to motivate students, especially those young people who have decided that there is nothing important to work towards, seems logical. That's why rewards and punishments are so common in schools.

However, **punishments** become just another pain to avoid, further eroding the natural 'towards motivation' of the student. **Rewards** may start as a short-term substitute for a worthwhile goal, but they soon backfire. If gold stars, treats or certificates are always offered, there soon comes a time when young people will not make any effort unless there is a reward at the end of it.

In the short term, this makes it challenging for a teacher to keep up the flow of incentives for these young people – a challenge that becomes increasingly difficult as they get older. In the long term, these youngsters become habituated to making no effort unless there is an immediate benefit. This works directly against their ability to delay gratification, which is one of the most important capabilities a child, or adult, can acquire.

# ~ SECTION 9 ~

## FEEDBACK AND FEEDFORWARD

9.1

## ☑ ADOPT

### FEEDBACK AND SELF-EVALUATION

In the process of developing student self-management, feedback and self-evaluation are strongly connected.

1. **Feedback** (and *feedforward*) provide students with information about how their learning and self-management are going, and how they can be improved.
2. Learning to **self-evaluate** empowers students to make their own assessments of their behaviour, and to adjust their actions without needing feedback from the teacher.

The interplay of intention and outcomes from feedback makes this a far more challenging aspect of teaching than it sometimes seems. Used carefully, the various aspects of feedback are very powerful instruments for enhancing performance and self-management. Used carelessly, they can undermine student confidence and achievement.

As this image suggests, feedback has the potential to provide:

- *Useful feedback and feedforward.*
- *Opportunities for young people to develop self-evaluation skills.*
- *Enhancements to their learning and self-management.*
- *Encouragement.*

Each of the strategies in this section emphasises one or more of these aspects of feedback.

As the diagram below illustrates, teaching young people to self-evaluate reliably, depends on them learning how to connect their internal processing with external references – especially with the feedback they receive from trusted adults.

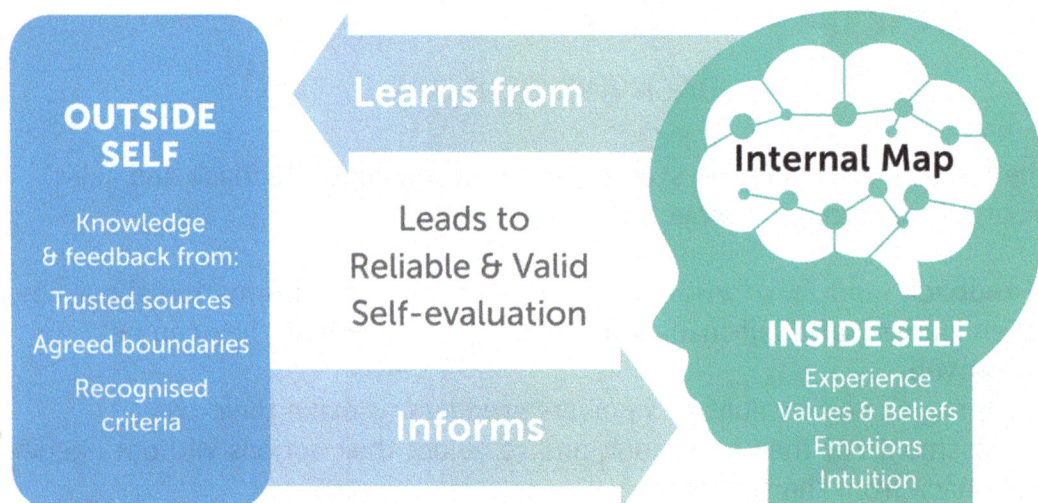

When the external references are **trusted** and are a **source of supportive feedback**, the student is more likely to accept those sources and to use them in their internal processing.

As you will see, the last two strategies in this section are focused on giving feedback because an important feature of learning to use feedback well is learning to give it.

Note:
**Feedback** provides information about what has happened. It is the rear-view mirror. *Feedforward* provides information about what to change or improve in the future (see 9.2). Feedback and *feedforward* are often linked, but all useful feedback should include an element of *feedforward*.
Remember that encouraging students to be self-managing applies to their learning and achievement goals - not just their behaviour. The same feedback and self-evaluation practices apply holistically.

## 9.2

### ☑ ADOPT

*FEEDFORWARD* THAT IS ACTIONABLE AND USEFUL.

Congratulations give the students a 'pat on the back' but are not necessarily useful. This kind of general recognition and appreciation of a student's work by a significant adult can be beneficial if it complements and supports the **internal motivation** for status and significance.

However, congratulations are not as useful as *Feedforward.*

The most useful feedback is actionable. If we give feedback about something that can't be changed, it has no useful purpose: (feedback about a completed assignment is useless unless similar skills and processes are needed again within a short time frame!). Information about an assessment that can't be improved is not very helpful. At its worst, it can lead to a negative self-judgment as in 'I am a 'D' student.'

The alternative is *feedforward*: a focus on a future behaviour that might help the student perform to a personal best level.
- *Feedforward* is always upbeat (here is how you can do even better / this is a step forward and the next step is..).
- *Feedforward* is optimistic (I believe you are capable and will keep improving).
- *Feedforward* is future-focused (it refers to what the student will do next or in future).

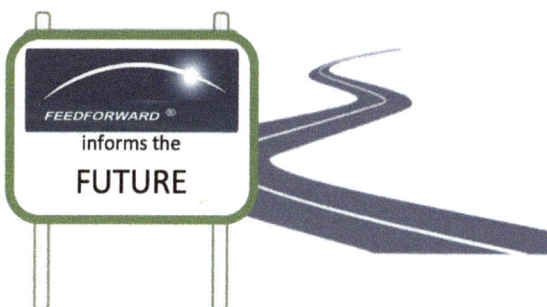

**FEEDFORWARD ®**
informs the
**FUTURE**

*Feedforward* and *Performance FeedForward* originated in the work of Rob Stones and July Hatswell, as a way of drawing attention to the future-focused dimension of what is normally described as 'feedback'. Feedback is of little use unless it informs the future – hence *Feedforward.*

Carol Dweck's research[1] is evidence that when young people receive *feedforward* about their performance that is **behaviour-specific** and shows that their performance is amenable to change, their self-image grows. They begin to see that there are powerful ways for them to improve performance and that today's achievements do not set limits on the future.

As students learn to receive and use *feedforward*, their ability to self-manage and adapt their learning and behaviour improves, as does their ability to self-evaluate accurately and reliably.

## 9.3

☑ **ADOPT**

**CLARITY ABOUT WHAT TYPE OF FEEDBACK YOU ARE GIVING.**

There are usually 4 Feedback types in the classroom :
1. Feedback about the progress or completion of **tasks**. (WHAT)
   'You have written four very clear paragraphs' or
   'Your answers show that you understand this kind of problem'.
2. Feedback about the **processes and procedures** used in learning. (HOW)
   'You set out your work very neatly and clearly' or
   'You carefully followed the step-by-step process that I recommended'.
3. Feedback about **self-management**. (HOW)
   'I noticed how patiently you stuck with the task' or
   'Thank you for letting other students take a turn'.
4. Feedback about the student's **personal qualities** (SELF)
   'You are very clever' or 'You rarely make much of an effort'.

The first three types provide information. As teachers, we must be clear about what the feedback refers to so that students can be sure about the aspect of their work that they can improve.

---

[1] Carol Dweck: 'Mindset'. Random House, 2007.

The fourth type is judgmental and, as Carol Dweck[2] maintains, implies that achievement or lack of it is due to personal qualities rather than to a variable that can be improved. Variables such as effort, use of procedures, and clarity of understanding, are amenable to change. Personal qualities such as being 'clever' or 'slow' are easily mistaken for features of a young person's identity.

With the development of a mindset that implies that things can't be changed - that I am either 'clever' or not, a 'good student' or not, someone who is a 'delight to teach' or not - comes debilitating helplessness. It's easy to give up when you think that things can't be changed!

Recognising that a growth mindset supports self-management reminds us to be very aware of the kind of feedback we are giving. My golden rule is that feedback and *feedforward* must be a source of **HOPE**. When students believe that things can get better and that they are in control of their learning and achievement, they are encouraged to self-manage.

**Our understanding of motivation tells us that we respond when there is a gap between what we want and what is happening (Section 8.5). This means that we notice deficits much more easily than the many good things that are happening.**

That is why it is essential to be alert for **positive *feedforward*** as well as 'corrective' feedback.

## 9.4
## ☑ ADOPT

### SUBSTITUTE *FEEDFORWARD* FOR GENERAL PRAISE

Specific congratulations or *feedforward* are always preferable to praise.

There are two reasons for this:

---

[2] Carol Dweck: 'Mindset', Random House, 2007.

1.  Praise conveys approval but not information. It is certainly not valueless. Edward Deci's research[3] shows that an approving comment from a respected teacher has a quite different effect from a reward. Teacher commendations do not interfere with intrinsic motivation. However, they are even more valuable when the feedback is informative as well as complimentary.
2.  Praise tends to be teacher-centered. In praising students phrases like 'I am proud of you,' or 'I think this is wonderful work' are often used. The focus of these opinions is the teacher. These kinds of evaluative comments are incompatible with the development of self-management. They put the teacher at the centre of judgments about the student's work and behaviour.

Compare: 'I am proud of you' with 'This is work that you can be proud of'.
The two comments have very different connotations.
Similarly, 'I am so impressed with this work' is not as useful as 'Your problem-solving skills are developing well'.

The first comment of each pair is all about the teacher's judgment. In the second comment of the pair, the reference is to the student and their work.

Students are more likely to develop their self-management if they perceive themselves as working towards their personal best as defined by either their internal criteria or agreed external criteria than if they are working to please their teacher.

This, like some of the other changes we can make when giving feedback, seems nuanced - small shifts in language and meaning. However, the effects are cumulative.

FEEDFORWARD ®

---

[3] Edward L Deci &Richard Ryan: 'Intrinsic Motivation and Self-Determination in Human Behaviour', 1985

# ☑ ADOPT

## APPRECIATIVE *FEEDFORWARD* TO CREATE AN OPPORTUNITY FOR SELF-EVALUATION.

*Feedforward* can be structured so that it is appreciative as well as informative and invites a self-evaluation.

## The process

Make an appreciative comment: 'I noticed the way you managed yourself / how well you persisted with that task / the quality of the work you did / the efforts that you made / the outcomes you achieved,'(whatever is appropriate). Use feedback that emphasises the task, outcome, process, effort, or self-regulation. Avoid personal judgments or superficial praise.

1. Provide your own very specific feedback in the form:
   **This is what I perceived and why I think it represents excellent practice or personal best performance.**

2. Ask: "What did you think about your own work or efforts?"
   **This is the self-evaluation question.** Useful feedback should include this opportunity for self-evaluation. Wait for - and listen to - the response. Knowing what the other person believes about their performance will help you to shape your future *feedforward*.

3. If a learning conversation follows from the first three parts of the feedback process, the teacher can use it to build further trust and understanding with the learner.

An example might be:
'I paid particular attention to the way you used adjectives in your description of the forest. You used lots of different words to emphasise how gloomy it was, and you created a very forbidding picture of a dangerous place.'

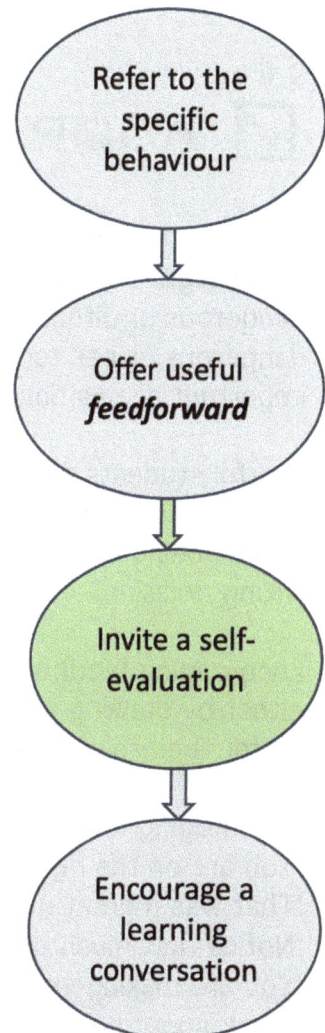

Refer to the specific behaviour

Offer useful *feedforward*

Invite a self-evaluation

Encourage a learning conversation

'What did you think of the effect you created? Did it come easily, or did you have to work hard to find the right adjectives?'

In the learning conversations that followed, the teacher might ask about the other writing genres that use vivid descriptions, and also about what the student has learned that will help them with future writing.

*Note:*

This is a thoughtful process. However, in practice, it need not be a long conversation. Even a brief conversation is much more productive than making a written comment on the work. It is the *shape* of the conversation that is important, and once this shape has been learned it can easily become a habit.

## 9.6

## ☑ ADOPT

### ENCOURAGING FEEDBACK

**Encourage** is one of my favourite words. Courage is the ability to tackle dangerous or difficult things. In our classrooms, which can be difficult and dangerous places for some of our students, the promotion of courage is such an important disposition.

Fearful students are rarely prepared to manage themselves. To accept responsibility for self-regulation requires the willingness to take responsibility, as well as being prepared to take the risk of giving the wrong answer or making the wrong decision.

Encouraging feedback is designed to persuade students to feel more confident, either by drawing attention to occasions when they were right or dared to stand up for themselves, or by challenging their self-doubt.

Encouraging feedback might be:
'You are on the right track again.'
'That was a great question that you asked.'
'Notice how much progress you have made.'
'You are making improvements each day.'
'Think about how well you persisted with that task.'

'When you speak up, you make a useful contribution to the discussion.'
'Your hard work is paying off.'
'It was great that you handed in the assignment by the due date.'
'That showed that you have tremendous determination.'

Notice that these comments draw attention to what a student can do or has done. The *feedforward* in encouraging feedback is focused on building confidence. It is intended to let the student know: 'You can do this!'

Encouraging feedback is one occasion when we can use some self-feedback. Because we are trying to enhance the student's self-esteem, this is a rare opportunity to morph descriptive feedback such as: 'You showed great determination in completing this assignment' into self-feedback such as 'That shows what a determined person you can be!' While generally following Carol Dweck's advice[4] not to make evaluative comments about the young person, challenging a negative self-perception can be an appropriate way of encouraging them.

Similarly, **disputing negative beliefs** can also be encouraging, especially when they draw the student's attention to a counter-example. Challenging a young person's belief is much better framed as a question than an assertion. For example: 'How will you find out how much you can do?' is better than: "You can do it!"

Some examples might be:
'Is the belief that you can't do Maths hurting you or helping you? Did you notice that you just completed four problems correctly? What does that tell you?'

'Where did the idea that you don't ask good questions come from? You asked me a really important question this morning.'

'What is the evidence for that discouraging belief (that you always need help)? Have you ever finished your work on your own?'

'What might change if you were to make up your mind that you are capable of completing this?'

'Where does that belief about not being able to spell come from? Is it always true? Have you ever spelt a word correctly?'

---

[4] Carol Dweck: 'Mindset' ibid.

Remember that discouraging beliefs are irrational but can easily become habitual. Challenging these beliefs with rational questions such as: 'Has there ever been a time when you were successful?' is effective, but it may take time for the habit to change. To speed things up it can be helpful to suggest an alternative belief: 'What if you were to always tell yourself that you can achieve whatever you are prepared to put effort into?'

## 9.7

## ☑ ADOPT

### PEER-TO-PEER FEEDBACK and *FEEDFORWARD*

Teaching students to give feedback or **feedforward** to each other is a highly effective way to teach them how to improve their work.

This powerful practice is most easily implemented when students are all working on an assignment that has clear criteria for success. Applying these criteria to each other's work helps them to understand what the criteria mean, and how the standards attached to the criteria are applied.

When the assignment is set:
- The criteria are explained, and the students are encouraged to begin the work.
- Once they have begun working and engaging with the expectations, the teacher can provide a model assignment at an 'A' and a 'C' level, and students work in pairs to decide which is the 'A' sample and which is the 'C'.
- They can then explain to each other what the differences between the samples are, and how these differences are related to the criteria.

With this understanding, the students are much better placed to self-evaluate their work as they go along. This enables them to improve the quality of their work as they are writing. The next step is for the students to confer with each other at the draft stage to highlight the way each does or does not meet the standards for each level.

Finally, before the completed assignment is handed to the teacher, a peer review of the final draft will allow the students to polish their work.

Peer-to-peer evaluations of this sort have 3 effects:
- They refine the students' understanding of the criteria and standards.
- They encourage students to keep refining their work until it is 'Quality'.
- They provide the students with the opportunity to develop and refine trust in their judgments – an important step in self-regulation.

Peer-to-peer feedback can also be used when students are working out how to evaluate their own behaviours against the boundaries established by the class. Students can be paired and asked to coach each other and give feedback about the degree to which they are choosing helpful behaviours, displaying patience, cooperating with others, or managing any other of the desirable behaviours in the classroom.

Using each other as peer coaches can help students understand the objective nature of the boundaries set and can take a great deal of the potential emotion out of the assessment of self-management.

For example, when students are doing group work and the noise level has become intrusive, instead of asking the students to work more quietly OR asking them 'Is the noise level helping us to work productively?', the teacher can say to the students: 'Please check in with your peer coach about how each of you is controlling the volume of your conversation.'

# ☑ ADOPT

## STUDENT FEEDBACK TO THE TEACHER

Possibly the most important step in creating a collaborative classroom in which the students take as much responsibility for classroom productivity as the teacher is for the teacher to invite helpful *feedforward* from the students.

As with every aspect of developing student self-management, some teaching is required here. The teacher should explain that there are criteria that should be applied to this *feedforward*. The reason that we want this information from students is to help us teach in a way that is most helpful to them. To keep improving our teaching it's valuable to know what is working best for the class.

Because students can be self-conscious about giving feedback until they get used to it, a good introductory strategy is to give each student a 'post-it' note in the last 3 minutes of the lesson and ask them to write on it:
- One thing they enjoyed or found helpful.
- One thing they would like the teacher to change or improve on.

As the students leave the classroom, they 'slap' the post-it note on the door.

Geoff, a colleague who taught me this strategy, told me that the secret to effectiveness is:
- At the beginning of the next lesson, mention some of the positive feedback that was received and say: 'Thank you'.
- **Make at least one change** that was suggested and tell the students that you are doing this.

Once students have got used to 'post-it' feedback, they become less self-conscious about offering feedback to the teacher, who can then move on quickly to ask the class to give them helpful feedback whenever they feel it would be beneficial.

Geoff told me that whenever he was unsure about the students' understanding, or about their ability to apply what he was teaching, he stopped and asked the class to give him feedback.

Sometimes teachers to whom I talk tell me that they are concerned that students will give them hurtful or personally challenging feedback if they invite comments from them. It's an understandable fear, but as another colleague, Greg, told me, receiving challenging feedback is often an opportunity for a teaching moment.

Greg, a teacher of history, recounted an incident from his own experience. He was accustomed to asking for feedback, so he asked his Year 9 class, early in the school year: "Are there any ways in which I can improve my teaching for you?"

One Student responded immediately: "You are boring!", he said.

Nervous laughter rippled around the room! The students waited to see how Greg would react. He thought for a minute and then replied: "Thank you. I certainly don't want you to be bored. Can you tell me specifically what I am doing that you find boring?"

The student squirmed a bit. He had not expected to be taken seriously and questioned like this. "You talk too much", was his reply.

"Tell me about 'too much'?", Greg replied. "It's going to be hard to teach you if I don't talk at all, but 'too much' implies that I am sometimes talking when I should be doing something else." He paused. "Let's bring in the rest of the class and ask everyone the question: "When do you notice that I am talking when I could be doing something else that would be more helpful to you?"

A few students rushed to reassure Greg that what he was doing was fine for them. He nodded and said with a smile: "Thank you for that. Now my self-esteem is not completely shattered." There was more laughter. He went on: "But this is important. If I sometimes keep talking when it would be more useful if I stopped and gave you time to think, or to ask questions, or to write a summary, then I need to know that."

Another student said immediately: "That would help me. You do give us so much information sometimes that I get a bit lost." Quite a few students nodded or murmured in agreement.

"Thank you", said Greg. "That's really useful feedback. I love history so much that I can get carried away." He paused. "Perhaps you can all coach me. When you need me to allow you to process what I am saying, by asking questions or summarising with a partner, can you give me the 'hands up' signal to let me know?" There were lots of nods. "Let's do that then," said Greg. "I will remind you from time to time that I will appreciate that kind of information from you."

Greg turned back to the student who had told him he was boring. "Thank you for starting that discussion. It's been very helpful. Only one thing, not just for you but for everyone: Can you see how what I call 'self' feedback is not specific enough to be useful? When we give each other feedback we should try to make it specific enough so that the person we are giving information to knows what to do about it."

Everyone nodded. The teaching moment had been exploited. Greg had been given a chance to model the way to receive feedback, and to remind the students about the need to provide specific information. Relationships had been enhanced rather than damaged.

Greg's wrap on the story was succinct: 'The only mistake we can make when we ask for feedback is becoming defensive. If we are open and accepting, then there is always a win-win outcome.'

# INTRODUCTION TO SECTIONS 10 TO 12

The next three sections are tied together. It is important to understand the relationship between them.

**SECTION 10:**
**Working it out** is the process used to redirect a student and restore a relationship after things have gone wrong. In the classroom, these processes are usually used to bring a student back inside the boundaries.

**Working it out** is a mature process that treats incidents of irresponsibility as problems to be solved. Everyone makes mistakes. Students learn from their mistakes. **Working it out** is an essential strategy in teaching students to self-manage.

**SECTION 11:**
**TIME-OUT** is a strategy that gives a teacher and student the time to talk through a problem and come to a resolution. It's often difficult to create an opportunity for time-out in the classroom, but when this is possible, it is desirable.

When there is a classroom incident, **TIME-OUT** can be used to let emotions settle and enable both the teacher and the student to bring their best self to the subsequent working-it-out conversation.

When **TIME-OUT** includes a temporary relocation away from the classroom, it may be a **logical consequence** of the teacher's initial lack of success in resolving a difficult situation quickly with a student. TIME-OUT should **never be used as though it is a punishment**.

**SECTION 12:**
**DEBRIEFING** is an opportunity for both a teacher and a student to reflect on what has occurred. Debriefing is a reflective process that aims to deepen the understanding of how incidents and mistakes occur, and how to avoid them in the future. Debriefing is usually crucial after any extended period of **TIME-OUT**.

DEBRIEFING is always about deep learning. It promotes recovery, reconciliation, and recommitment to greater understanding and responsibility.

# ~ SECTION 10 ~

## WHEN THINGS GO WRONG - DEALING WITH INCIDENTS

However well most students are managing themselves most of the time, there will be incidents. Even when you are very effective in teaching students to behave responsibly, and even when they usually behave cooperatively and manage themselves responsibly, there will be incidents. Students (and teachers) can make mistakes. Learners of all ages can be side-tracked from self-managing by circumstances, or by their own emotions and physiology.

In these circumstances, teachers need strategies for **working it out** to get back on track, calm the classroom and restore their relationship with a young person who has not been behaving responsibly.

## 10.0
## ☑ ADOPT

### WORKING IT OUT

When students behave irresponsibly or interfere with your teaching in any way, adopt the practice of **working it out**.

When you encounter resistance, rudeness, or rebellion, it's your job to remain calm, confident and in control. Whatever you do, avoid the temptation to get angry or get even! This is a teaching moment - a chance for you to model self-management.

There are three issues to be addressed in working it out:

- The immediate issue of a disruption to the teaching and learning process.
- The problem of the student behaving in a way that is outside the agreed boundaries.
- The harm done to the relationship between the teacher and the student.

The Relationships Knot

The issues are logically different but emotionally entangled. The **relationship 'knot'** has to be unpicked!

The teacher is dealing with a behaviour that is outside the boundaries, so they must be firm and act decisively without resorting to threats. The student is usually behaving impulsively or wilfully rather than responsibly, so their behaviour threatens both teaching and learning and also the relationship with the teacher.

Dealing with these complexities is always challenging, but it is made easier if the teacher recognises the situation as problem-solving and has a suite of trusted practices to call upon, especially if the situation escalates.

When a teacher knows that they can simply follow effective procedures without getting into a 'win-lose' conflict, it is easy for them to remain calm and confident.

## 10.1
## ☑ ADOPT

### WORKING IT OUT #1

Use a short series of intervention questions. This is a 30-second process aimed at nudging the student back to responsible behaviours.

The teacher moves close to the student and, in a calm and supportive tone, asks:

"Lucas, what are you doing?"

*"Nothing."*

"I thought I saw you trying to take Sarah's book. Is that inside the boundaries or outside it?"

*"I don't know."*

"It's outside." The teacher continues without a pause: "Do you know what work I have asked you to do?"

*Lucas nods his head.*

"Do you know how to do it?"

*Lucas nods again.*

"Can you start now? Thank you."

**The teacher walks away**.

This is a standard short intervention. The teacher's part is almost all questions. The teacher's tone never changes. The body language is calm and relaxed. The teacher does not enter into a dispute about whether Lucas did or did not try to take the book. If the student denies taking the book, the teacher uses the **broken record**[1] strategy and repeats, without changing voice tone or volume: "It seemed to me that you were trying to take Sarah's book. Would that be inside or outside the boundary?" - then waits for Lucas to answer the question.

The 'walk away' strategy is deliberate and tactical. It signals that the exchange is over and that the teacher has no interest in a confrontation or 'a battle of wills'.

If the teacher attempts to establish their ascendancy with a glare, or by standing and waiting to make sure that Lucas starts work, the student is invited into a public battle of wills. What has been an invitation to take responsibility becomes a public contest, with the class as an audience. The best way to end the interaction is the two-part 'statement' by the teacher:

**"Thank you". Walk away.**

Notice that the aim of working it out #1 is to encourage the young person back to on-task learning as soon as possible.

---

[1] Broken record is a simple assertiveness strategy that usually does not escalate the potential conflict. By repeating the same information or instruction without raising their voice or changing tone, the teacher maintains their position in a boringly insistent way!

## 10.2

### ☑ ADOPT

#### WORKING IT OUT #2

If the student's disruptive behaviour continues, the next level of intervention is still **very short**.

There is no change in tone or body language. The teacher again moves close enough to keep the exchange private and asks:

"Is there a problem Lucas?"

*"I can't do this stupid work?"*

"Oh, I see. Do you know what to do when you are stuck?"

*"I need help."*

"What did we agree that you should do if you need help?"

Sulkily: *"Put my hand up."*

"That's right. Putting your hand up lets me know that you want help. Can you do that?"

*"I suppose."*

"That's great. Now I know that you need help, I will get to you as soon as I have helped Ahmed and Simone."

*"Why can't you help me first?"*

"Well, as we discussed, putting up your hand puts you in the queue. Then everyone is helped in the order that they ask for it. Just jump in the queue." (The teacher raises their hand to remind Lucas how to do this).

The teacher says: "Thank You" and walks away.

Once again, the main focus of the strategy is to encourage the student to return to productive work as soon as possible.

When these first two strategies do not improve the situation, a longer conversation will be necessary.

## 10.3

## ☑ ADOPT

Have a one-on-one conversation with the student. If you can make the time in class or if you are close to a break period, have this conversation as soon as possible. If you need more time, you can call for executive support to enable you to have this conversation (See TIME-OUT #3)

1.    **Ask the student to identify and STOP the behaviour that is creating some disruption to the learning.** (*'What are you doing?' 'Is that helping me to teach or you to learn?' 'Can you please **STOP** what you are doing and work out with me something that you can do instead?'*).

2.    **Listen to the student's perception of the situation.** Take their perception seriously and respond to any concerns that they have. However, if they are outside the boundaries, don't accept any excuses.

3.    If they air a grievance or say that you are picking on them, don't argue with their perception. Instead, agree that you are paying them special attention and promise them that you will discuss these issues, but that now is not the time. At this point, you are asking them to choose a replacement behaviour that will allow you both to continue with the class activity.

4.    Attempt to negotiate a replacement behaviour that is inside the boundaries and that will satisfy the Basic Needs just as well as the unhelpful behaviour. (If you suggest a behaviour that is likely to diminish their sense of status or sense of fairness, they will either not agree, or agree but not stick to the agreement).

5.    Negotiate a good plan with the student. One that:
      .......is acceptable to both student and teacher.
      .......has a realistic chance of success.
      .......is attractive and specific.
      .......can be practised if necessary.

**6**  Determine the next step:
   a) Implement the plan that has been negotiated.
   b) If the plan doesn't work, the student will be required to go to a
      TIME-OUT space until you can have a longer discussion.
   Traditional classroom management tends to focus only on
   only Step 1 ....
   'Stop that! And if you don't ............'

If disruptive behaviour continues, you will need a still longer conversation. Use your judgment about whether that is possible in the classroom or if you will need a 'Time-Out?' (Section 11)

## 10.4

☑ **ADOPT**

WORKING IT OUT #4

If the short intervention fails, focus on the boundaries.

> Say, for example: "I think we have a problem. Can we work this out?"
> If they are willing to talk, ask the student: "Do we have a boundary about calling out?" (or whatever the relevant boundary is).
> Whatever the student answers, whether they identify the boundary or reply something like *'I don't care about your stupid boundaries',* go on with:
> "When we talked and agreed about not calling out, what did you think we meant?".

> Notice that you are asking a 'thinking' question to move the young person onto their 'front wheels' and away from their 'emotional wheels'.

> Whatever the student answers, keep focusing on "What do you remember about our discussion about the boundary" or "What does this boundary mean to you?".

When the student has identified the relevant boundary and what it means, ask them "Can we work out how to get back inside the boundary?".

You can then 'future focus' the conversation on the positive behaviour the student can display that will take them back inside the boundary.

There is no remonstration or accusation about what the student was doing 'wrong'. The focus of the conversation is on where the boundary is and how to behave in ways that are inside it. Keeping the conversation at this level means that the student does not feel the need to be defensive, or to justify what they have been doing.

## 10.5
## ☑ ADOPT
WORKING IT OUT #5

This strategy depends on establishing an agreement with the school's executive staff that allows you a few minutes to '**work it out**' with the student. With this agreement in place, you can call for support while an executive member or support staff member takes the class, allowing you to spend some time with the student.

If you have this agreement in place, as soon as it becomes clear that a longer conversation with a student is needed for you to work it out, you can call on executive support. When the support person arrives, take the student away from class to a place where you can have an uninterrupted conversation using 'Work it Out' #4.

My preference in this situation is to walk slowly, side-by-side with the student. Walking slowly makes it easy to slow the rhythms of the brain so that you are both in a reflective mood. Walking side-by-side is a useful conversational posture for problem-solving because there is no chance of confrontational eye contact.

An alternative is sitting side-by-side. Having worked with indigenous students who try to avoid eye contact anyway, I often found myself seated on a bench and drawing in the earth with a stick. Beside me, the young person would be doing the same. This matching of behaviour and body language makes it far easier to work it out because rapport is enhanced by matching physiology.

Use either of the extended 'work it out' strategies (10.3 or 10.4) for this longer conversation.

## 10.6

☑ **ADOPT**

### WORKING IT OUT #6

**This step is for the teacher to take when they have a little reflective time away from the class.**

Take a few minutes to reflect on your interaction with the student. Focus on what you have been doing, not on what the student has been doing.

i.   Make a list of the things that you have done when the student is behaving irresponsibly.

ii.  Ask yourself candidly: 'Is what I have been doing with this student working?' If the answer is no, then make a commitment to change those behaviours and make a new start with the student.

iii. Make a plan to send clear signals to the student that you want to work with them in a positive way. You might plan to say to them: "My job is to help you and to be the best teacher I can be for you. When it's not working out like that, I would like each of us to do something for each other that will send clear signals that we both want to make a new start."

iv.  When you next meet with the young person ask: "What can I do to show you that I am serious about improving things between us?" (Note – don't agree to anything that is **outside the boundaries.** Do agree to anything that is **inside the boundaries** and that will make things better.)

v.  Ask the student what they will do to send you a clear signal that they want to improve things between you. (It might be as simple as giving you a 'thumbs up' next time they are 'on task'.) Agreeing on an interim signal between you is a way in which the student can show you that they intend to make changes, even though they may not get it right immediately.

## 10.7

☑ **ADOPT**

**Remember that all behaviour is purposeful.** Your unsuccessful interaction with the student is often somewhere downstream of the incidents and experiences that created their attitudes. Understanding how they perceive their own behaviour and intentions can be a longer-term way of addressing whatever the student is perceiving and experiencing – and a good way to get you both on the same side.

When you and the student have the time, conduct a deeper exploration of the purpose of the student's behaviour by using these questions:

**Say: "Things have not been working well for either of us in the classroom. How do you see the situation?"** Listen empathically to whatever you hear.

**Ask: "If things were working for you, and if you were feeling safe and successful in my classes, how would it be different?"** (Explore whatever the student says. Don't offer solutions at this stage - remember that you want the young person to feel in control. Help them to achieve clarity about what they want by asking questions such as: 'What would that mean to you?' or 'How will that improve things' when they identify a positive 'want'.)

**Ask: "Is what you are doing getting you what you want?"** or "Is it likely to lead to the outcomes you want?" or "Is this the best way to get what you want?" or "Is there a better way?" or "Is what you are doing helping you or hurting you?".

**Ask: "What else can you do?"** or "Is there a better option?" or "Can we find a way to get you what you want and at the same time look after the learning needs of everyone in the class?" or "Have you noticed what other students do which works well in the same situation?".

Notice that it is not useful to ask the student why they are behaving irresponsibly because this can easily be interpreted as a request for an excuse. Young people are rarely able to explain their deeper motives. However, they can share their thoughts. When led through these problem-solving questions, they can usually work out what can be done to improve things.

## 10.8
☑ **ADOPT**

### WORKING IT OUT #8

Use this process when you want to be reconciled with a student after a breakdown in your relationship.

1. Focus the conversation on **the outcome you want -** a more pleasant and supportive relationship between teacher and student. Keep this outcome in mind and steer towards this result wherever the conversation leads. This first step is important. If you allow yourself to be side-tracked by what you as the teacher **don't want**, or use the conversation to air grievances, then the reconciliation will probably not be successful.

2. Manage your voice tone and body language throughout the conversation. Be as calm and open as you can. (Imagine that you have an audience that you would like to impress with your demonstration of skill and self-control.)

3. Anticipate what the student will be concerned about or blame you for and begin by apologising or conceding these things. This step takes the wind out of the young person's sails and enables the dialogue to move quickly into the positive. A good way to approach this is to agree with the effect that any conflict may have had on the student, but make it clear that this was not your intention.

4. Explicitly future-focus the conversation. Say: "I know things have gone wrong in the past, and we can't go back in time and fix them. We can only change the present and the future and that is what I hope we can do."

5. Use Fogging* (next page) if you feel criticised. E.g. 'It may have seemed as if I did that at times but that was not my intention, and I would like to make sure that in the future......'

6. Show that you are listening intently to what the young person wants and agree with whatever you can. Whenever there is something that you can agree with, say so explicitly. This step is the magic bullet!

7. Complete the conversation by summarising any commitments each of you has made.

# ☑ ADOPT

## FOGGING – AN ASSERTIVENESS SKILL

Fogging is an assertiveness strategy that helps us deal with manipulative or public criticism from others.

Imagine that you are a dense bank of FOG into which the 'slings and arrows'[2] of other people's critical comments can be absorbed and vanish without a trace! The FOG has no feelings and never responds. Whatever enters the FOG vanishes into the grey mist!

**CRITICAL COMMENTS** > **FOGGING** > **COMPOSED RESPONSE**

Here are the key steps to Fogging:

o  Avoid denial of the critical comment or 'put down'.
o  Smile.
o  Take the key words from the comment and use them in your response by **agreeing** with anything that might possibly be true (even if all you can agree with is their perception).

Student: You expect too much of me!
Fogger: *I do have high expectations of you.*

Student: You are being unfair to me!
Fogger: *I try to treat every student in the same way, but I am probably not 100% successful.*

Student: You are picking on me!

---

[2] William Shakespeare: 'Hamlet', Act1 Scene 3

Fogger: *I probably am paying a lot of attention to you at the moment.*

Student: You are so bossy.
Fogger: *I do try to get my own way when I believe passionately in something.*

As you can see, FOGGING does several things. First, it forces us to listen to exactly what the critic says (in order to use their words in our response) but without defensiveness. It also enables us to accept feedback in a composed manner and to give the critic food for thought without replying in kind.

A good FOG has an element of re-framing to it. It accepts the 'criticism', but without feeling the need to retreat from the position which initiated it. If you have a habit of being defensive in the face of criticism, it will help if you learn this strategy and absorb everything into the FOG.

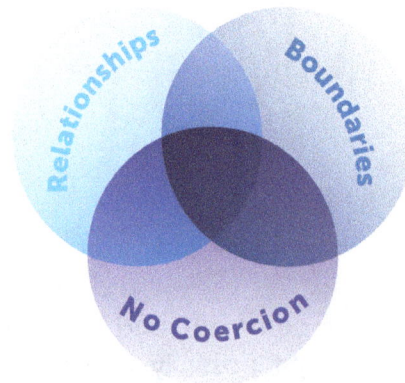

# ~ SECTION 11 ~

## TIME-OUT FOR LEARNING

☑ **ADOPT**

### WHEN TIME IS NEEDED TO HEAL A SITUATION

TIME-OUT is a sensible and useful process whenever time is needed for **working it out**.

When there is insufficient opportunity to **work it out** in the busy bustle of the classroom, teacher and student may need some space and time to create an opportunity for the longer conversation they need to have. Whenever there has been an incident that has not yet been resolved, or which damages the relationship between student and teacher, time is often needed for resolution and healing.

TIME-OUT may need to be taken as a consequence (**i.e. result**) of a situation when a student and teacher have not had the opportunity or time to work out the issues between them. **It should never be confused with a punishment!**

In some schools, TIME-OUT is misunderstood and treated as a kind of banishment. Students are 'sent' somewhere to be fixed or told to 'get out' until they are allowed to return. It is easy to slip into this way of seeing TIME-OUT. In most incidents, the student is outside the boundaries, and as a consequence of something that they have done or said they have to **work it out** with the teacher.

It is appropriate for the teacher to communicate that the student will have to find a way back inside the boundaries before they can resume their normal place in the class. It is reasonable to delay the conversation between them until there is time and space to **work it out**.

## 11.2

### ☒ AVOID

#### USING TIME-OUT IN ANGER OR AS A PUNISHMENT

The sequence of **working it out, TIME-OUT and reflection is educative**. Used properly, these behaviours promote student self-management. They help young people learn how to recover and repair when they make a mistake. If they are used punitively, then the logic of the sequence is lost on the student and the purpose of the TIME-OUT will be distorted.

## 11.3

### ☑ ADOPT

#### USE TIME-OUT WHEN IT TAKES LONGER TO WORK IT OUT

When the time you need to talk with a student is not available in the course of a normal lesson, use one of the 'TIME-OUT' strategies that will allow both you and the student to work things out positively.

The classroom is suited to short interventions. When extended conversation with the student is needed, longer interventions, away from the 'audience', are often necessary.

When 'TIME-OUT' is necessary, make sure that it is not initiated in any way that makes it seem like a punishment. 'TIME-OUT' should be used as a procedure that allows for a deep discussion when there is insufficient opportunity during class time.

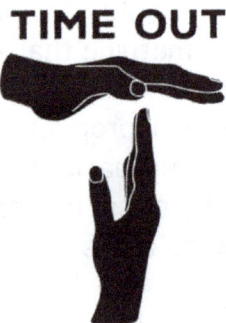

**TIME OUT**

☑ **ADOPT**

### TIME-OUT FOR LEARNING #1

Position a table and chair somewhere in the classroom that will be out of the way of other students OR just outside the classroom (if the age of the students and school policy allow it). Name this the 'TIME-OUT' space. Explain to your class **WHY** a TIME-OUT space is sometimes needed.

When you need a TIME-OUT to allow an opportunity to resolve a classroom situation, it's important to be careful with your words and tone. For example, say calmly and respectfully: 'I think there is a problem that we need time to work out here. Please go to the 'TIME-OUT' space until we have a few minutes to talk.'

Speaking like this supports your goal to help students self-manage. It would **sabotage your purpose** to snap out: 'That's enough! Go to the TIME-OUT space now!'

When the student has moved to the TIME-OUT desk, take a moment to make sure they have something to do. If it takes a while for you to make time to talk with them, I recommend that you check in with them from time to time to let them know that you have not forgotten them and to explain why you have been delayed.

## 11.5

## ☑ ADOPT

### 'TIME-OUT' FOR LEARNING #2

When the student will not go to the "TIME-OUT' space, or when they continue to distract or disrupt when in the space, **call on school executive staff** to take your class for a few minutes while you talk with the student.[1] This strategy is the same as that outlined in **Working it out** #5.

'TIME-OUT'#2 gives you and the student a few minutes to work out the problem between you. This is an opportunity for you to invite the young person to take responsibility and to help them to find a replacement behaviour. You can use the questions from 'Working it out' in the previous section.

This is a very different approach from sending the student to the Stage Leader, Head of Department, Deputy Principal or Principal. Referring the student to be dealt with at an executive level usually backfires in two ways:

- It does not improve the situation. The student who was uncooperative and stubborn in your class will usually be cooperative and agreeable in the Deputy Principal's office. In that context, there is no problem. However, when they come back to the classroom nothing will have changed and you will not have been included in the positive interaction between the student and the Deputy Principal.
- It signals to the student that the situation is too difficult for you to deal with and this diminishes your authority.

'TIME-OUT' #2 enables you to have the in-depth negotiation that you and the student need to help them take responsibility and find a replacement behaviour that will work for them.

---

[1] Executive staff will almost always be ready to adopt this strategy. They know that they have no power to 'fix' the student for you and will usually be delighted to support you in this way. Of course, they also lead very busy lives, so they may not be available when you need them. In that case, you may have to move to another level of TIME-OUT.

## 11.6

☑ ADOPT

### 'TIME-OUT' FOR LEARNING#3

**'TIME OUT' #3 is the best option available when neither of the two strategies above has worked.**

When you use 'TIME-OUT'#3, you ask the student to go to a different location to wait until the two of you have an opportunity to talk. Let them know that you will meet with them as soon as possible.

In 'TIME-OUT' 3 you are simply **parking** the student in an alternative space with a warm and supportive person who will provide the student with some reflective time, or with an opportunity to continue their work on their own. Depending on your school arrangements, this alternative may be a desk in another teacher's classroom, with an executive staff member, a guidance or counselling specialist, or in a dedicated TIME-OUT space.

As soon as possible, meet with the student to use one of the working-it-out procedures. It is important to do this at the earliest possible opportunity.

Even if you are having an exceptionally busy day, try to call on the student at the TIME-OUT space to see if they are ready to talk with you, and to schedule the first available time.

## 11.7

☒ AVOID

### USING 'TIME-OUT' AS A PUNISHMENT

Avoid using 'TIME-OUT' as a punishment or thinking of it as a solution. 'TIME-OUT' is simply a holding space that allows you to keep teaching the rest of the class until you have time for a **working-it-out** conversation.

Many schools set up a 'Time-out room', 'Reflective room', 'Planning room', or 'Responsible thinking room', believing that this space will somehow be a 'solution' to irresponsible student behaviour. In many of these supervised spaces, students are required to fill in a form that asks them to answer the **'working it out'** questions while they sit and wait. **This is not a helpful or legitimate use of 'TIME-OUT'!**

The breakdown of order in the classroom is almost always partly a **relationship** problem between the teacher and the student. When it can't be resolved at the time by one of the 'Working it Out' conversations, then it should be addressed at the earliest possible opportunity. Nothing is gained by delaying and letting the situation fester in the mind of either teacher or student.

## 11.8
## ☑ ADOPT

### TIME-OUT FOR LEARNING #4

'TIME-OUT'#4 moves the need for a time and space for negotiation to the school-wide level. It is only necessary when:
- The student refuses to engage in a **'working it out'** conversation with their teacher.
- After **working it out** and TIME-OUT strategies have been attempted, the student will not agree to choose behaviours that are inside the classroom or school boundaries.

At this level of TIME-OUT, the school will need either a dedicated person or a dedicated space to manage the situation. A person who will talk supportively with the student and try to persuade them to agree to work it out with their teacher is the preferable option. If a space is provided but there is nobody available to talk with them, schoolwork should be provided so that the student does not fall too far behind.

If the school is a High School, or there are specialist lessons as well as their normal class, the student should attend those lessons. The TIME-OUT only applies to the class in which a negotiation with the teacher is incomplete.

This kind of TIME-OUT should not be prolonged. As soon as the student agrees to have a conversation with the teacher, then that meeting should be arranged.

# ☑ ADOPT

## TIME-OUT FOR LEARNING #5

This level of TIME-OUT will involve the student staying home from school until they agree to a **'working it out'** conversation and a return to responsible behaviour in the classroom. This level of TIME-OUT **should never be used** if the student is willing to talk with their teacher.

This is not the same as a formal suspension from school. A suspension is used when a student has been involved in unsafe or antisocial behaviours that are unacceptable in the school setting. Students who are suspended are **outside the school boundaries**. Because of the legalities involved, suspensions are often for a set period.

TIME-OUT #5 is not the same as a suspension. If the student is ready to return immediately, then this TIME-OUT can be very short. I have experienced many situations when a student who would not agree to **'work it out'** with their teacher changed their mind after 10 minutes of discussion with a parent!

Essentially, TIME-OUT#5 is terminated as soon as the student and parent agree to the student returning to the classroom via a **working it out** discussion with their teacher.

In this situation, the school will insist that in addition to a **working it out** conversation with the teacher, a DEBRIEFING conversation will also be needed.

{NOTE that a DEBRIEFING conversation should always be held after a suspension, as well as a **working it out** discussion with the teacher involved in the issue that led to the suspension. Like a TIME-OUT, a suspension will not change a student's behaviour. It is the conversations that they have on their return to school that can lead to more responsible behaviours.}

## 11.10

### ☒ AVOID

#### RETURNING A STUDENT TO CLASS WITHOUT A REMEDIATION PROCESS

A student who has been suspended or has had a lengthy period of TIME-OUT for some reason should **never** be returned to class without the teacher being involved in a restorative conversation.

The next chapter sets out a number of practices that can be used to restore the relationship between student and teacher and ensure that **learning** is the outcome of the time of separation.

# ~ SECTION 12 ~

## USE RESTORATIVE AND EDUCATIVE DEBRIEFING

### 12.1
☑ ADOPT

#### DEBRIEFING 1

**What did you learn?** (What did we learn?) is a very simple recovery strategy after a behaviour incident. There is no hostility or blaming in this question.

The implicit assumption is a very healthy one for wellbeing in general. 'What did you learn?' presupposes that from every experience, even those that do not go well, there is something to learn.

**What did we learn?** This form of the question includes the teacher. Once again, it invites a neutral evaluation of what has just happened. Asked in a calm or inquiring tone it invites both the student and the teacher to think about what happened and about what each might change in the future.

### 12.2
☑ ADOPT

#### DEBRIEFING 2

**Listen and Paraphrase** is another way of helping the student review and reflect on a behaviour incident. Ask them to tell you what happened as a narrative: what started things off?, what happened next?  At each step, try to understand what the student means[1] by what they say and paraphrase their thinking in a non-judgmental way. Even if their narrative includes a criticism, or if they blame you or another person, paraphrase it as the way they were thinking at the time. Remember that this is **their** story!

When they have told their story and feel heard, you can gently ask some reflective questions.

- What was most useful about what you did?
- What was most unhelpful about what you did?
- Was there any point at which doing something different would have changed how things turned out?
- If you could re-tell that incident and change some of what happened, what would you need to change in order for things to have turned out well (or at least better)?

---

[1] This is the 'Second Perceptual Position', a very useful paraphrasing skill for teachers. See the next page.

## 12.3
☑ **ADOPT**

### DEBRIEFING 3

Use the 'Perceptual Positions' to reflect on the situation that has occurred. It is sometimes useful to explain the Perceptual Positions before you begin.

**FOURTH**

**Broad Perspective**

In this position, I am focusing on the importance of good relationships and general well-being in the classroom.

**THIRD**
**Observer**

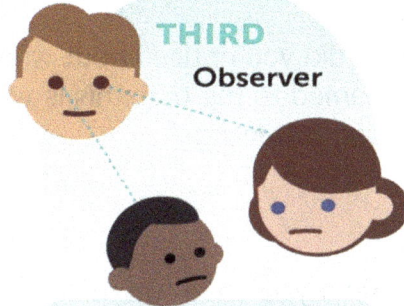

In this position, I am trying to see what happened through the eyes of a neutral observer – somsone who is watching but not taking sides.

**SECOND**

**You**

In this position, I am seeing the situation from your point of view, doing my best to imagine how you were thinking and feeling.

**FIRST**

**Me**

In this position, I am thinking my thoughts, feeling my feelings and seeing things from my point of view.

In your conversation with the student, start at the First Position and work through each of the other perceptual positions in turn. Always ask for the student's perception first, then add your own.

S is the question from the teacher to elicit the student's perception.
T is the teacher's perception.

### 1st Position
S      "How did you see things?". "How would you describe what happened?".
T      "This is how I saw the situation and is my interpretation of what took place."

### 2nd Position.
S      "What did you notice about what I was thinking or feeling?".
T      "It seemed to me that this is what was happening for you – how you were thinking or feeling?"

### 3rd Position.
S      "Pretend you were watching the situation from the viewpoint of a neutral person in the classroom. What would they have seen and heard?".
T      "If I take the position of a neutral observer, the things I would have noticed were...."

### 4th Position.
S      "What do you think will need to happen to improve the situation, now or in the future? What will these two people need to do to improve wellbeing in the classroom?".
T      "I think that what each person could do to improve the situation and for both to feel positive about the classroom is ....."

When the teacher and student have visited and shared their perspective in each of the Perceptual Positions, they ask each other:

**"What will you do to improve the situation?"**

**Note:** It often helps to set out a physical space for each of the four perceptual positions with a number on a card.

As you go to each of the Positions, stand next to the space.

When you have visited all four Positions, walk back to Position 1 and ask each other the question:

**"What will you do to improve the situation?"**

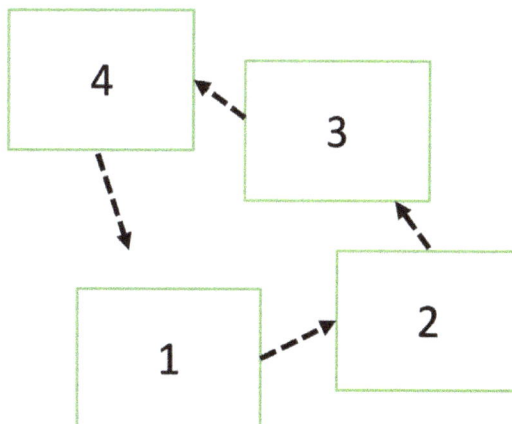

```
        ┌─────────┐      ┌─────────┐
        │         │      │         │
        │    4    │ ←--  │    3    │
        │         │      │         │
        └─────────┘      └─────────┘
             |                ↑
             ↓                |
        ┌─────────┐      ┌─────────┐
        │         │      │         │
        │    1    │ --→  │    2    │
        │         │      │         │
        └─────────┘      └─────────┘
```

## 12.4

☑ **ADOPT**

**THE STOP TOOL[2]**

The STOP tool is a more elaborate process for debriefing an incident that helps the cognitive brain to connect with physiology and emotion in reviewing a situation. It's a way of learning how to interrupt the conflict cycle.[3] When used as a debriefing practice, it helps the student use a whole-body response to understand how they lost control, and where they can take better control in the future. When the debriefing phase is over, it can be used as a way of practising a whole-body response in similar situations.

The STOP TOOL is based on the behaviour car metaphor for teaching students about how their mind works. (See the 'How the mind works' Section 8.)

> **The third page of Section 12.4** has a template from which you can cut out seven cards that can be laid on the floor in the arrangement illustrated.

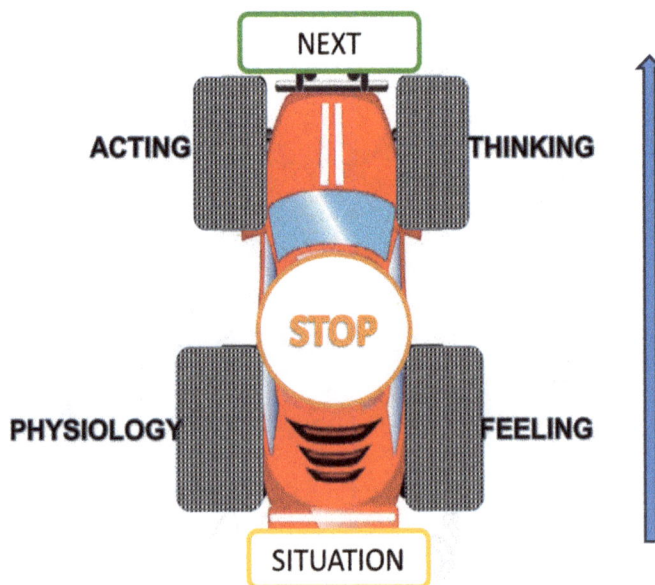

---

[2] The STOP TOOL evolved from an activity created by Dr. Ali Sahebi and Judy Hatswell, using the car metaphor.
[3] Nicholas Long: 'Managing Highly Resistant Students', *Perspective*: Spring 1990 or see the website of the 'Life Space Crisis Organisation': https://www.lsci.org/conflict_cycle

## Stage 1

Commence the debrief by inviting the student to stand on the 'Situation' card and ask them to describe the situation that initiated the incident **as they saw it**.

Then ask them to stand with one foot on each of the 'Feeling' and 'Physiology' cards and describe how they were feeling and what their body state was at the time.

Then by-pass the STOP and ask them to stand with one foot on each of the 'Thinking' and 'Acting' cards and describe the thoughts and actions that followed.

Finally, ask them to stand on the 'Next' card and describe the consequences (what happened next) of their actions. At this stage, there is an opportunity to discuss the negative consequences of the incident and why it would be best to avoid these consequences in the future.

## Stage 2

Ask the student to go back to the start and stand on the 'Situation' card again. You can say: 'We are going to re-run the script as before, but this time through we are going to use the STOP to plan a better 'next' (a better consequence).

Once again, ask them to stand with one foot on each of the 'Feeling' and 'Physiology' cards and describe how they were feeling and what their body state was in the situation that you are reviewing.

**Now say: "STAND on STOP".** Before you move again, let's discuss what the ideal way to resolve this situation could have been. What would have happened at 'NEXT' if things had gone differently and you were really pleased with your self-control?

When the student has described a 'next' that would have been better than what actually occurred, ask them to stand on 'Thinking' and 'Acting' and describe the thoughts and actions that would lead to the desired result. Then have them step onto 'Next' and describe the ideal or preferred result again.

## Stage 3

Repeat several times. Every time the student runs through the STOP part of the process and makes a decision about what to think and do to get a desirable result, they are contributing to the re-wiring of their own brain and forming a new habit.

The STOP strategy is the centrepiece of many cognitive therapy techniques for improving self-management. This version is particularly useful for young people because:

- It embraces the part that feelings and physiology play in students' actions and thinking.
- It is a kinesthetic strategy that combines doing and thinking.
- When repeated, it can help a student acquire useful automatic thoughts.
- It can be used as a small group activity for the whole class.

**The 'STOP TOOL' template is on the next page.**

# STOP TOOL TEMPLATE

**STOP**

**Situation**

**Next**

- ACTING
- THINKING
- FEELING
- PHYSIOLOGY

## 12.5

☑ **ADOPT**

## The Solving Chairs[4]
**a process for mediation**

Suppose the relationship between the student and the teacher has reached a point where the differences between them are interfering with learning and wellbeing in the classroom. In that case, this mediation process may be required. The mediator can be a colleague of the teacher or a member of the school executive who has the respect of both the student and the teacher.

If the way they are relating to each other is a problem for the teacher or student - or both of them - then the 'Solving Chairs' process can be a very effective way to help. However, each has to be **genuine** in their recognition that their relationship is hindering them and that they want to improve it.

The procedures are:

1. Invite the two people involved to a mediation process. Set up two chairs at $120^0$ to each other and take the third seat facing these two.

2. Invite the teacher and the student to sit on the chairs as a sign that they genuinely want to get on better with each other and work more productively together.

3. When they are seated, the mediator explains that in any working relationship there are three entities – the two people themselves and the relationship (or

---

[4] Based on 'The Solving Circle' – a process developed by Dr. William Glasser, interpreted by Rob Stones

the 'way they get on' together). The mediator will guide them to talk about the 'way they get on with each other' not *about* each other. Emphasise that this is critical to the success of the process.

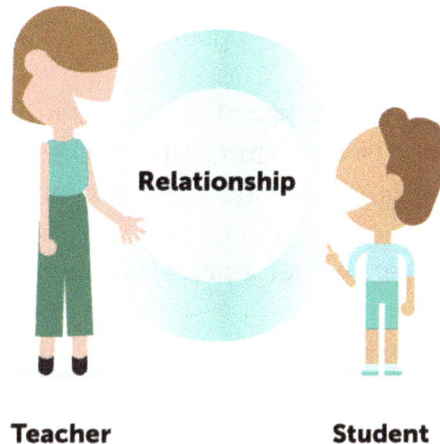

Teacher          Student

4. Ask each of them in turn what they believe to be the problem with **the way they are relating as teacher and student**. Caution each of them that they are not to say what they believe is wrong with the other person – this is not a blaming exercise. They are to focus on the relationship itself and explain briefly what they think is wrong with how they are getting on with each other. (Participants will often have difficulty with this: seeing the problem in the relationship as solely 'the fault of the other person' is deeply embedded in the thinking of many people, young and old.) The mediator may have to interrupt the conversation if either the teacher or the young person criticises or blames the other person  - and refocus them on the third entity: the relationship.

5. When both have identified one thing that is not working in the way that they are relating, the mediator asks each person "Whose behaviour can you change?" Wait for each of them to answer.

6. Now each of them is asked to speak about one thing that is positive about the way they work together or have worked together when things were going well.

7. The mediator asks each person what strengths that they believe they bring to the way that they work together.

8. And then the mediator asks: "Will each of you tell the other person one thing that you are prepared to do in the next 24 hours that you think will improve the relationship?".

9. During the next week, each is asked to plan one **additional** thing that they can do to improve the working relationship in the future. This will be discussed when they meet again (after a week has passed).

10. Each is also asked to do a third thing – a sort of extra signal that you want things to be better. 'During the next week will you each do one thing that you have not mentioned here to improve the relationship?'

11. Agree to meet again after the time period specified.

**Note:** This process can also be used to mediate between student and student, or teacher and teacher. It is not useful for mediation between groups.

## 12.6

☑ **ADOPT**   DEBRIEFING 6

## INTRODUCTION TO NEGOTIATION

Negotiation involves two people with different wants or goals moving towards an agreed solution.

Negotiation is tricky for a teacher and a young person because it is difficult to reach a productive solution if the balance of power between the negotiating parties is unequal. For a successful negotiation to occur, the teacher will have to agree to negotiate in good faith and as an equal party.

When we are negotiating we have to plan our approach carefully.

- The 'hard approach' is competitive and often only satisfied by 'winning'. The assumption here is that the value being negotiated is fixed. Anything gained by one party is a loss for the other. This is counterproductive and almost always damages the relationship.

- The negotiator who chooses a 'soft approach' is prepared to lose in order to reach an agreement – but the feelings associated with 'losing' may damage the relationship in the future.
- The 'relationship-centred' approach is focused on 'both-win' by finding ways to create shared value in the solution. If 'both-win' is not possible, a compromise may be found that will still support the relationship.

The 4 'classic' negotiation outcomes are illustrated below:

| | | Student | Teacher | |
|---|---|---|---|---|
| Both student and teacher get what they really want. The relationship is enhanced. | | Win | Win | |
| A solution is found in which each gets something they want. The relationship is stabilized. | | Compromise | Compromise | |
| Either teacher or student gets what they want and the other loses. The relationship is compromised. | | Lose | Win | |
| Neither teacher nor student will budge, and the fragile relationship is not improved. | | Lose | Lose | |

## 12.7
## ☑ ADOPT DEBRIEFING 7

## NEGOTIATING 1- FOCUS ON 'WHY'

When two people disagree, questions need to be asked that focus on the **reasons** for their different positions, or the **purpose** that each attaches to the situation.

Marco Korn's[5] 'Alignment Triangle' below illustrates the importance of resolving these **WHY** issues in a negotiation.

Focusing on 'what I want you to do, and how I want you to do it' will almost always deepen the disagreement. **Most stubborn disagreement is focused on specifics – on HOW things should be done.**

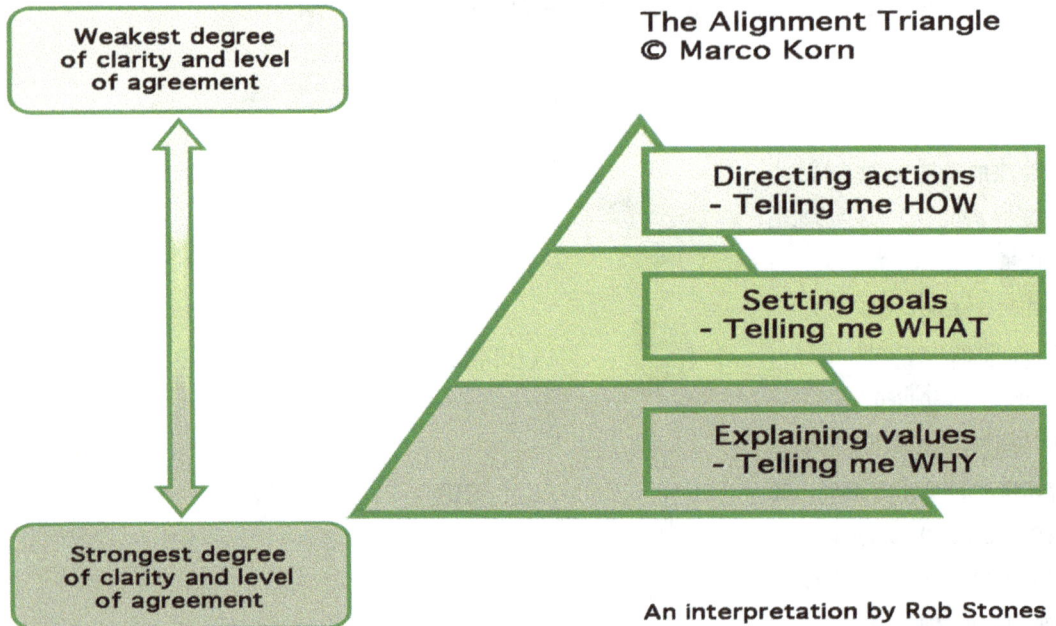

**Weakest degree of clarity and level of agreement**

**The Alignment Triangle © Marco Korn**

**Directing actions - Telling me HOW**

**Setting goals - Telling me WHAT**

**Explaining values - Telling me WHY**

**Strongest degree of clarity and level of agreement**

**An interpretation by Rob Stones**

In the negotiation, the teacher should focus on: 'why I want you to do this' or on the value both will get from working together?' This will tend to move both of you towards agreement.

Questions to the student should be: 'Tell me why this is important to you?' or 'What does your 'want' mean to you?'.

This style of negotiation does take some time, but because it is value-orientated it leads to more sustainable resolutions of issues, and to deeper levels of restoration of the relationship.

---

[5] Marco Korn is a Brisbane-based Psychologist who specialises in dispute resolution.

## ☑ ADOPT DEBRIEFING 8

## NEGOTIATING 2- USE SPIRALLING

This style of negotiation is helpful in clarifying what each person wants and WHY they want it.

The two people in the negotiation take turns to ask each other the following six questions that spiral towards the deepest level of the common value that will resolve the issue.

- What difference will it make if you get what you want?
- What will improve in our work together if we both get what we want?
- What will it mean to you to get what you want?
- What's important about getting what you want for us to be working together productively?
- How will you feel if we can find an agreement that suits us both?
- What will it say about you if we can work this out together?

Using this process helps the teacher and the student to clarify what each really wants and will open up more options for a 'Win-Win' outcome.

It sometimes helps to write the student's answers into one circle in the Venn Diagram below, and the teacher's answers in the other.
Anything common or similar goes into the shared portion of the diagram.
The aim is to bring everything that is significant into the shared area - the area of agreement.

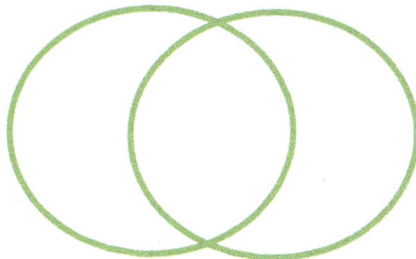

# ~ SECTION 13 ~

## QUALITY

### 13.1
### ☑ ADOPT

### DEFINE QUALITY WORK

When we teach students about their 'Quality World' (Section 8), we can easily go on from there to initiate a discussion about 'Quality Work' if we use a classroom meeting (Section 6.4).

Drawing from what students know about the Quality World, we can use the '**define**' part of the conversation to draw out some criteria that help us identify Quality Work:

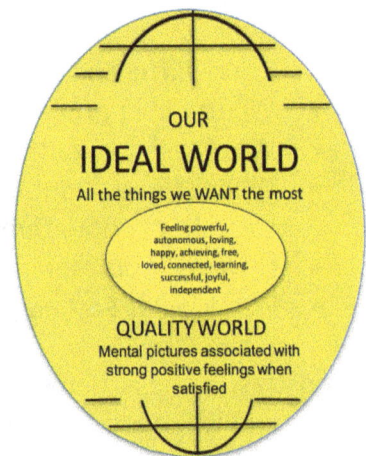

OUR
**IDEAL WORLD**
All the things we WANT the most

Feeling powerful, autonomous, loving, happy, achieving, free, loved, connected, learning, successful, joyful, independent

QUALITY WORLD
Mental pictures associated with strong positive feelings when satisfied

  - Quality has a personal dimension - it is work that we feel proud of.
  - Producing Quality Work feels good.
  - Quality Work is our 'personal best'.
  - Quality Work is meaningful or useful.
  - Quality Work is the best that we can do.
  - We often have to improve our work to achieve Quality.

We can move on from the 'define' phase of the conversation to **personalise** the student's thinking:
'What does producing quality work mean to you?' or 'How do you feel when you produce Quality Work?'.

Then we can use a **challenge** question such as:
'What prevents us from producing Quality Work?'.

Once students have achieved some clarity about what is meant by Quality Work, we can begin to make Quality the standard that students are aiming for whenever work is to be evaluated.

As you will read below, aiming for Quality, and using strategies that emphasise all aspects of Quality, is relatively straightforward in the early primary school years. As we move into the secondary phase of schooling, when comparative assessment is required by the school system this becomes more complicated. (See Sections 13.5 & 13.6).

## 13.2
## ☑ ADOPT

### QUALITY IS USEFUL OR MEANINGFUL

It is very difficult to produce Quality Work when the task or assignment is mundane, or when students can see no relevance in the work. One of Dr Glasser's expectations of a Quality School is that students are only asked to do 'useful work'. This is not only work that as adults we deem likely to be useful in the future; it refers to work that seems useful or meaningful to the student in the present moment.

> I remember being asked to take a Year 9 'learning support' class for an absent colleague. The work set for them consisted of filling in the blanks on a worksheet. It tested their recall of some basic information about transport. It was quickly apparent that the work was neither interesting nor challenging. For a while, I went around the class encouraging them to make progress. Then I looked around and took in the body language of the young people. They were slumped, lolling about in their seats with only a few actually writing.
>
> "Please stop what you are doing!", I asked. "Please bring your chairs outside and make a circle of chairs in the shade of the tree."
>
> When they were all seated I asked: "Can you tell me why you were not finding that worksheet on transport interesting?"

I was immediately overwhelmed by comments from almost all the students expressing their opinion of the work that had been set for them. "It's boring!", "It's all obvious.", "They ask us to do this stuff because we are dummies.", "It's all useless!" were among the opinions that they called out.

I calmed them down and asked them to speak one at a time. These are the questions I asked, and the answers I received. After I chose one person to answer, I asked who agreed with them and invited other comments so that nobody in the class of 16 students was left out.

"Why do you think you are being asked to do this work?"
"Because we are the dummies class. Nobody thinks that we can do the same work as other kids."
"How do you think the work you are doing compares with what students are doing in a mainstream class?"
"Their work is harder." "They are allowed to talk to each other." "They get more assignments." "I was in an ordinary class and I could get help from other kids."
"What would happen if you were asked to do the same work as a student in the other classes?"
"I think we would need more help, but it would be interesting." "We might fail at some things, but not everything." "The work would be harder, but not so boring."
"What do you think are the main differences between your lessons and the lessons being taught to students in other classes?"
"The students in other classes get more choices." "They get more respect!" "They have more students in the class." "The teachers just teach the smart kids and we get left behind."
"If I were your teacher, what could I do to keep you interested and encourage you to do your best work?"
"Have discussions like this." "Give us more difficult things to do but help us when we get stuck." "Give us more choices about how to do the work."
Finally, I asked: "Can you work in threes and make suggestions about other ways of telling your teacher what you have learned about transport?

The students worked busily until the end of the lesson, making suggestions such as 'draw all the different kinds of transport', 'make up stories about catching planes or driving cars or trucks', 'find out as many ways as possible to transport stuff from here to somewhere else in Australia.'

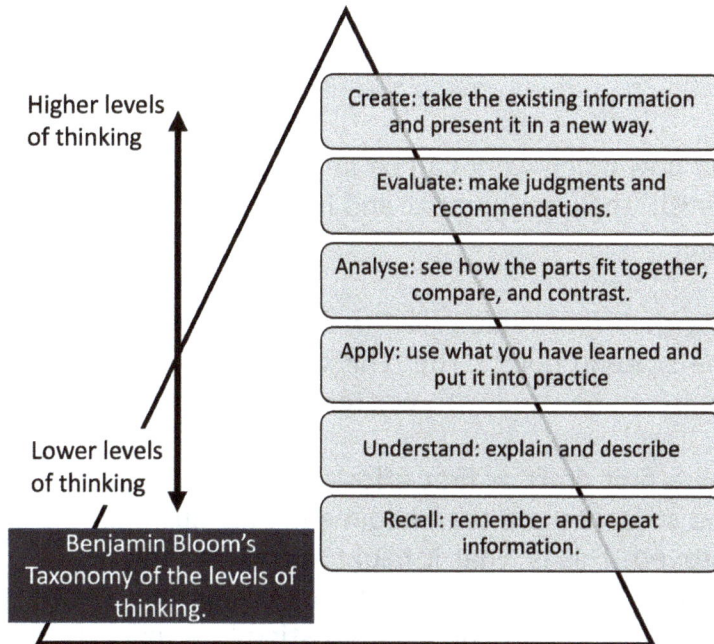

Higher levels of thinking

Create: take the existing information and present it in a new way.

Evaluate: make judgments and recommendations.

Analyse: see how the parts fit together, compare, and contrast.

Apply: use what you have learned and put it into practice

Understand: explain and describe

Recall: remember and repeat information.

Lower levels of thinking

Benjamin Bloom's Taxonomy of the levels of thinking.

As you have probably noticed, the questions I asked the students required them to recall, understand and explain, apply their knowledge, compare, make recommendations and be creative.

If we use Bloom's Taxonomy, then we would say that they were quite comfortable with using both lower and higher-order thinking in comparing their experiences with those of other students in the school. It was not necessary, and very uninspiring, to fill in worksheets that offered only the lowest level of thinking – remembering and filling in the blanks.

The point I want to make is that almost all students can work at levels that feel like quality to them: levels of thinking that enable them to make sense of the world and be challenged to reason and reflect.

If we aim to encourage Quality Work in the classroom, especially in High Schools, we should avoid pre-judging what students can do. If we want all students to aspire to Quality then the kind of work we ask students to do must require them to access the highest level of thinking and presentation that they are capable of.

## 13.3

☑ **ADOPT**

### THINK OUT LOUD and MAKE TIME TO EDIT

The '**THINK OUT LOUD**' strategy is an effective way to model a key dimension of Quality Work – editing, refining, and improving the first draft of the work.

When they don't understand how much work can be improved when it is reviewed, many students 'finish' their assignment and hand it in – often without even reading it through again.

Teach students that creating their first draft is like their first attempt at mastering a skill: it's just the starting point.  The 'Think out Loud' strategy is based on teacher modelling. It can be used with written, oral, or skill-based work, but the pattern is:
-   The teacher produces a first draft or first effort.
-   They share it with the students and then begin a monologue about how the draft can be improved. This is what it might sound like: my first sentence is  'I am going to tell you about my Christmas. Is that the best way to begin? It doesn't sound particularly interesting.' I wonder if I could turn it into a question such as 'Would you like to hear about my crazy Christmas?'. That might be a bit better ..... or what about something a bit dramatic? I could write 'The dog ate the turkey, the Christmas lights caught fire, and that was just the start of my crazy Christmas....'
-   As soon as possible, draw the students into the editing process, taking their suggestions about what to say next. With every improvement suggested, the teacher modifies their work.
-   When the teacher and the students all agree that the work is the best that they can do together, the teacher puts a big 'Q' on the finished product and hands out copies to the students.
-   The students compare the finished assignment with the first draft. This is usually enough to convince the students that work can be improved.

The second part of the strategy is '**MAKING TIME TO EDIT**'.

The time that teachers set for a task or assignment to be completed varies widely, depending on the age of the student and the complexity of the task. However, to teach students to **first** make a draft and **then** edit their work, use the **'two-thirds/one-third'** rule.

1. A date is set for the first draft to be completed. This should be about two-thirds of the total time available for the project or assignment.
2. The remaining one-third of the time allocated is used for editing and improving the work, aiming for 'Quality' or 'personal best'.

Adopting this strategy usually helps students to get into the habit of planning their work in this way.

## 13.4
## ☑ ADOPT

### SELF-EVALUATION, CO-EVALUATION AND PEER EVALUATION

There is a process for teaching students to recognise Quality, even when it is their own work that they are evaluating. Until young people understand that they need to improve on their initial draft, they tend to simply hand in their first draft and say that it is the best they can do.

To help students evaluate their own work reliably, it helps if the teacher makes the criteria for Quality clear and emphasises that taking time to revisit and improve is an integral part of producing Quality.

Students can begin to practise checking this for themselves and then with a peer. In both cases, the students ask themselves or each other:
- What could be improved from the first draft?
- What has been improved from the first draft?
- Is there anything else that can be improved?

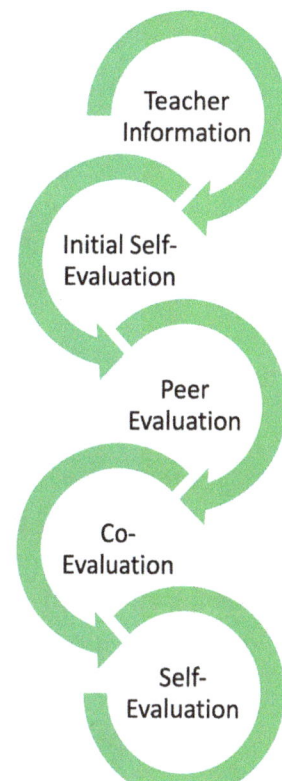

Teacher Information

Initial Self-Evaluation

Peer Evaluation

Co-Evaluation

Self-Evaluation

When a student is confident that the work is the best that they can do, they can ask the teacher to co-verify with them.

The teacher asks the same questions that were used in the peer evaluation – or uses the coaching questions (Section 14).

If they have more information that will enable the student to improve the work, this is the time to give it. If the work can be improved further then the student should be asked to improve it as much as they can.

Finally, the student is asked to confirm that the work is 'Quality' and write a 'Q' on it.

Once that process becomes routine, students become increasingly reliable in making judgments about whether their work is their personal best.

## 13.5

## ☑ ADOPT

### QUALITY AS THE PRINCIPAL STANDARD FOR CLASSROOM ACHIEVEMENT

Teachers are educators, but they mostly work in schools. Schooling is not the same as education! Schooling imposes limits and demands on education that can distort the way that teachers go about their work.

In every classroom, teachers aim to help students to learn as well as they can: to do their very best and to achieve Quality in all their learning outputs.

Quality is the best work that a student can do. Producing work of Quality feels good because it satisfies the student's need for competence, recognition, and achievement. Producing Quality Work is intrinsically motivating. When students are taught and their work evaluated in a way that provides them with the time and encouragement to do their best, Quality is always possible.

In primary years, the focus on Quality can remain the principal standard against which the work is judged. The young people are encouraged to compete against their previous best efforts, not against each other!

However, school systems require teachers to sort and grade students so that faster and more capable learners can be differentiated from those who are less capable and take more time and support to do their best. This is schooling. Schooling imposes hustle and comparison on the gentler nurturing process that is education.

When students are in the early years of schooling, this tension between individual achievement and comparative success is not so great. Students who are producing the best Quality Work of which they are capable are doing well enough to feel satisfied with their work. However, in the upper primary years and throughout High School, the emphasis on comparative achievement increases. This is not a problem for students who are achieving good grades, but it's all too easy for young people whose work is being compared unfavourably with others to perceive that they are not doing well and to lose interest in school.

This is one of the areas where teachers need to work at the very highest level of their subtlety and skills. They are faced with striking the balance between helping every young person to produce the best Quality Work of which they are capable, and the expectations of the school system that students be evaluated and graded against objective criteria and standards.

## 13.6

☑ **ADOPT**

### QUALITY-RELATED ASSESSMENT MANAGEMENT PRACTICES

Because producing quality takes time, students who are slower learners, or slower producers of learning products, often take longer to achieve their personal best work.

As students progress through the grades, the pressure to 'keep up' coupled with increasingly demanding timelines make it difficult to provide the time these students need to do their best work.

There is no mystery about why there is such a strong connection between disruptive behaviour and school failure. Young people cannot 'switch off' the need for achievement and success. Students who are not able to satisfy their power needs through school success in the comparative system become disconnected. If they are not even given the time to produce 'Quality', they will be tempted to explore ways of being powerful that are unhelpful in the classroom!

If they are expected to create the same amount of product and in the same time frame as every other student, they often have to hand in a task or assignment feeling rushed and frustrated. Not being able to produce work of a quality standard is unsatisfying and very disconnecting. The result is that these students lower their expectations and give up. They expect that however hard they try they will receive failing grades and not be able to work at their own personal best levels.

As teachers, we can help by suggesting adjustments to timelines and content in five ways:
1. Adjust the volume of work that students are asked to do so that they can achieve quality outcomes. It is usually more satisfying for a student to achieve a 'C' grade on work that they have done their best with, even though they have not tackled the parts of the assessment that would have given them access to an 'A' grade.
2. When students complete in-class assessments knowing that they have not done their best work, award a grade of NY (not yet) rather than a failing

grade. The student can keep working on the task and hand it in later when they feel satisfied that they have done their best.

3. Allow students to re-submit a piece of work if they have handed it in and been awarded a low grade that is not indicative of the best they can do. When they receive feedback on the work and realise that they could have done better, invite them to revisit the work before handing it in. Of course, this, like the previous strategy, requires students to commit extra time and effort. This is a choice that invites a student to self-manage in a situation in which self-discipline pays off.

4. Adjust deadlines for these students so that they can follow the procedures to produce 'Quality'. If the class has 6 weeks to produce an assignment, students who need more editing time to produce their best efforts can be asked to finish their draft in only 4 weeks. This sounds contradictory, but experience shows it can lead to more satisfying results. The outcome may be that many young people can achieve passing grades by spending less time on the draft and more time on editing. This is probably because they are used to being given a tighter structure by the teacher so this is familiar territory to them. (See Section 13.5)

5. Coach for Quality. Keep 'Quality' as the main focus of coaching for these students. They know that they are operating in a comparative system. However, their best chance of keeping up with that system is doing the best work of which they are capable. As a result, the work itself can be satisfying and meaningful, whatever 'grades' it is rewarded with.

# ~ SECTION 14 ~

## 14.1

☑ **ADOPT**

### GOAL-SETTING:
### A KEY SKILL FOR SELF-MANAGING AND ORGANISING TIME

Young people who set and achieve goals are more likely to manage themselves purposefully than those who don't. In addition to the academic benefits, and the contribution that goal-setting makes to delaying gratification, setting and achieving goals has a profound effect on personal wellbeing. Students who feel that they are in control of their life and studies are more confident and more organised than those who do not feel this way.

There are many ways in which a classroom teacher can help students with goal-setting:
- By developing rudimentary forward planning and goal-setting skills with those who have none.
- By stretching the capacity of those who already plan and set goals but could learn to do so even more effectively.

| SMART GOALS | |
|:-:|:--|
| **S** | **SPECIFIC** |
| **M** | **MEASURABLE** |
| **A** | **ATTRACTIVE** |
| **R** | **REALISTIC** |
| **T** | **TIME-FRAMED** |

Always try to guide students towards setting SMART goals, remembering that the 'A' in SMART stands for **attractive**. If students are persuaded, by parents or teachers, to set goals that are not appealing to them, they will contribute far less energy to those goals than when they set goals for themselves that will bring them pleasure through achievement.

As you read through the strategies below, match them to the capabilities that your students already have, and help them to take the next step.

The golden rule in teaching students to adopt goal-setting is that **it should be the student who sets the goal**. The teacher's job is to provide the scaffolding that will help them set and achieve their goals. When the teacher sets targets or goals for a student it can be experienced by the student as external control. When the student sets their own goals, they are practising internal control.

## 14.2
## ☑ ADOPT

### SIMPLE GOAL-SETTING QUESTIONS

Always have ready a suite of questions that will help students set goals and work towards achieving them:

- What is your goal?
- What's the next step?
- Do you have a specific target?
- What do you want to achieve?
- What would you like this project to look like when you have finished?
- How are you going to measure your success?
- What will feel like Quality to you?
- What will you be proud of?
- How many examples will you complete?
- How far can you go with this?
- How will you know when you are ready to show me your work?
- What would be a personal best for you?
- How hard will you push yourself to achieve something you will be proud of?
- What do you think you can achieve?

## 14.3
☑ **ADOPT**

### PERSONAL BEST 1 - TARGETS FOR PHYSICAL ACTIVITIES

When students are running, jumping, throwing, or engaged in any individual physical activities, ask them to set their own performance goals. Setting goals for a physical activity provides a very powerful metaphor for goal-setting in general.

Setting personal targets is very different from competing against other students!

For example, when teaching students to throw a ball or discus, (I was a Physical Education teacher early in my career), I taught the basics of the throwing action and then gave each student a peg and asked them to set an individual target. I explained that all performance is individual and that we all benefit from setting our own goals. I was not interested in a competition about who was able to throw the furthest.

Almost all students set conservative targets (no matter what skill level they started at), and most of them quickly exceeded these goals. As my teaching and coaching continued, I kept focusing on whether students could exceed their own **personal best** and, given that focus, most students persisted and kept improving.

Striving for **personal best** achieves very different outcomes from competition. When the same physical activity is set up as a competition, the 'pecking order' is quickly established, and students who are not doing well compared to their classmates quickly lose interest and give up.

I used the same principle for cross-country running. On the first attempt, I always told students: "It does not matter how fast or slow you are. On this first try, you are simply finding out how fast you can **comfortably** complete the course." Subsequently, the young people were simply challenged to see if they could improve on their first effort – even by a few seconds. I always published the list of times in two columns - with the first column and main focus being on how much students improved their previous time. Achieving personal best was the prized goal, and even the student with the slowest actual time could be the person who was celebrated for improving the most.

In the schools in which I worked, the cross-country season lasted six weeks. By the sixth week, almost every student was running all the way and showing pride in their improving achievement. Personal best is like Quality: it always feels good!

## 14.4
# ☑ ADOPT

### PERSONAL BEST 2 - CLASSROOM GOAL-SETTING

The best academic goal-setting uses the same focus as the strategy for achieving individual sporting goals: personal best.

However well a student is currently performing, in any area of their schoolwork, there is always an opportunity to do better. If a student starts at a very low level of performance, they will usually get a dopamine 'buzz' out of doing better.[1] Unless they are distracted by comparing themselves to students who are far more naturally capable, setting personal best and achieving it is motivating.

Dr Albert Mamary[2] gave a simple but elegant demonstration of setting the right kind of academic goals to a group of teachers at a seminar at The University of Central Queensland. He asked for volunteers to climb the steep steps of the lecture theatre with him. He asked each person to do their best to climb as many steps as they could in five seconds. They all set off, and after five seconds the timekeeper said 'STOP'. Al was on the eighth step. A teacher on crutches was only on the sixth. Two teachers were almost at the top, with the rest scattered at various steps below them.

What Al asked the participants was, "If we repeated this, what would be your achievable goal ?"

Almost everyone pointed to the step above themselves or the one beyond. Al's message was clear. Our job as teachers is to help the students set goals at the

---

[1] Dopamine is the body's natural reward system. When we anticipate a pleasurable achievement, the hypothalamus releases a small amount of this neurotransmitter into our bloodstream. It feels good! When we achieve success, more dopamine is released – it feels good again!
[2] Dr Albert Mamary was Superintendent of the Johnson City Schools in New York State in the U.S.A. He was a celebrated educator and an inspirational teacher.

next 'step' beyond their present level of performance. It would simply be discouraging if everyone were being compared to the two 'greyhounds' among us who almost reached the top.

Teachers who are skilled in the use of goal-setting as a tool are always focusing on each student's personal best. When they are speaking with individual students, they talk about setting incremental targets based on their last piece of writing, drawing or problem-solving. When they talk with the whole class, they talk about everyone achieving their personal best.

What we know as teachers is that having a goal enables a student to be actively engaged in what they are taught. Passivity is the enemy of learning! Everybody flourishes if students have a stake in what they are learning. Teaching students about setting achievable goals is powerful pedagogy!

Sometimes identifying 'personal best' means lowering the bar before the student can raise it.

I remember teaching Kathryn, a student in her first year in High School. As she came through the door for the first class of the year she told me: "I hate Maths."

Kathryn was not belligerent, she simply felt helpless. As she soon told me: "I have never passed a Maths test. I always get an 'E'."

What I had to do was clear. If I wanted Kathryn to change her belief, my job was to teach the next topic so well and make the test so accessible that she would be successful. I told all the students that it was simply to check their understanding of my teaching.

Kathryn got an 'A'! I returned the test papers to the students individually and watched her face as she looked at the grade on the paper. I could almost see her beliefs shifting. It did not matter to her that every student in the class got an 'A'. What mattered to Kathryn was that *she* did!

The next test was the normal end-of-term review test. I asked everyone in the class to set a personal best goal. I prepared all the students in the same way, with a normal amount of review and checking for understanding. Kathryn predicted a 'D' but achieved a 'B'. In the next three years, she expected to be (and was) successful in every Maths test she took. She chose the hardest level of elective Maths in Year 11. She told me: "It's not easy, but I know I can succeed if I have a goal and work towards it."

I tell Kathryn's story to illustrate the importance of the teacher's role in helping students set achievable individual goals **and then achieve them.**[3] No matter where they start, everyone can strive for their **personal best.** As students get used to the idea that they are competing only against themselves, they rely less on the teacher's encouragement and their motivation is internalised.

## 14.5
## ☑ ADOPT

### STEPS TO ACHIEVEMENT

There are two aspects to goal-setting. The first is to set the goal, the second is to achieve it.

Students will continue to set goals **if they achieve them**. This underlines the importance of teaching young people HOW to achieve a goal.

Especially when tasks are complex, it is important to break them into parts, and into a logical order so that students can work step-by-step to achieve the goal.

Teachers of younger students naturally break instructions into brief parts, like providing a recipe. This **'recipe for success'** approach is very useful in helping students to manage multi-part tasks whatever age they are. The key for the teacher is to work out whether the students can do this for themselves or not.

---

[3] I am not advocating lowering standards so that everyone can pass. Quite the contrary. I am recommending 'stretch goals' for everyone. However, there are times to lower the bar so that every student believes they can achieve the goals they set for themselves. We can learn from the training of whales at Sea World. These enormous creatures are first encouraged to clear a rope that is underwater. As they progress, the rope is raised gradually until the whale is jumping spectacular heights. Children, like whales, need to believe they can achieve small goals before setting themselves ambitious ones.

Some very young students come to an early understanding of the recipe for success strategy, but I often encountered students in Years 11 and 12 who had still not mastered this for themselves.

This is one of those aspects of teaching where the teacher's attitude to the learning process is critical. 'They should have learned this when they were in primary school.' is no help to the student who has not yet mastered a particular aspect of learning (or self-management). The most effective attitude to this situation, and to all aspects of self-management is that *now* is always the right time for students who have yet to learn something.

One of the most successful teachers I have worked with always asked the student: "Do you have a recipe?" or "Do you know how to get to your goal?"

## 14.6
## ☑ ADOPT

### MERGING LONG-TERM AND SHORT-TERM GOALS

An effective way of teaching students how to work towards their long-term goals is to draw attention to the **process** of achieving the goal. I sometimes used the following goal-setting and reflection process:

Students were asked to:
- Benchmark their present level of achievement. This might be a grade, but more often could be a level of skill that they felt they needed to improve.
- Identify a goal that would represent their new personal best – one step beyond what they were presently achieving.
- Write the goal on a sheet of paper and put it in an envelope that is then placed in their personal tracking file.

- Identify and write into their day pad the steps to this goal. Sometimes this might be the dimensions of the capability they want to develop. At other times it might be a habit they need to acquire to achieve success. (I always cautioned against being unrealistic. Steps to success, like goals themselves, must be **realistic, attractive,** and **achievable.**)

Periodically (usually twice a term) the students were invited to retrieve the envelope and check on their progress towards the goal - or revise the goal in discussion with me if necessary.

When progress towards the goal was being made, the students could confidently resume their plan. When the students were not making progress, they could revise their plan.

## 14.7
## ☑ ADOPT

### ASHER'S OCTOPUS

The Octopus is a way of using questions to promote goal-setting AND identify progress towards a goal. My colleague Mark Asher who designed this process used it with high school students who were a bit 'lost' and needed to be clearer about the connection between their present work and their long-term goals. It is a wonderful tool for this purpose.

However, I have also introduced Asher's Octopus to teachers of students from Kindergarten to Year 12 (and to the parents of young people of all ages). It seems to adapt well to the age and context of students across this wide range.

Please notice that this is not a worksheet to hand out to students! It works when used by a supportive adult who listens intently to what the student says and asks questions sensitively and responsively.

**PRESENT SITUATION** in as much detail as possible

PATHWAYS

**FUTURE GOALS** with as much attractive detail as possible

Most teachers start at the gold end of the diagram by asking the students to think about how they would like things to be. Depending on the circumstances of the conversation, the question can be posed about long-term goals or relatively immediate goals.

For example:

- A Year 9 student might be asked: 'How would you like to see yourself five years from now?' 'What would you like to be doing?' 'What would you like to be happening in your life?'
- A Year 4 student working on a Science task might be asked: 'How would you like this project to work out?' 'What would you like to be able to say about it when you have finished it?' 'What would make you feel proud of it?'

The conversation usually starts hesitantly, but as the teacher writes the student's thoughts into the gold circle (using the blank diagram below and on the full page) they usually become more engaged as their ideas are made visible. It's important not to rush this initial part of the conversation. It's the key to the process.

When the future goals have been written into the diagram, the teacher asks about the 'present situation': 'What is happening at the moment?' 'Where are you on the journey towards your goal?', 'How far have you got with this task or project?'

PRESENT SITUATION — PATHWAYS — FUTURE GOALS

When the 'present situation' has been established, the teacher and student begin to explore the pathways to the goal that are illustrated by the tentacles of the Octopus. These are the behaviours that will lead to the achievement of the goal. The pathways can be written into the tentacles if they both agree that they will lead to the goal. Behaviours that are likely to be 'dead ends' and detract from progress towards a goal can be written onto extra tentacles that can be drawn onto the diagram but are not joined to the desirable goals.

When the diagram has been completed, the student and teacher agree on which tentacles are most important in helping the student towards the goal, and then put a * against them.

Work through each of these to make sure that they are:
- **Specific behaviours** (not good intentions). 'What will I see you doing?' or 'What will I hear you saying?' are questions that help to make the pathway specific.
- **Measurable** in terms of tangible progress. 'What will change?' / 'How will we know you are making progress?'
- **Attractive** to the student. There is visible enthusiasm.
- **Realistic** – the student has the capabilities to pursue the pathways identified.
- **Time-framed** in that there is a completion date for stages of progress.

 THE ASHER'S OCTOPUS TEMPLATE

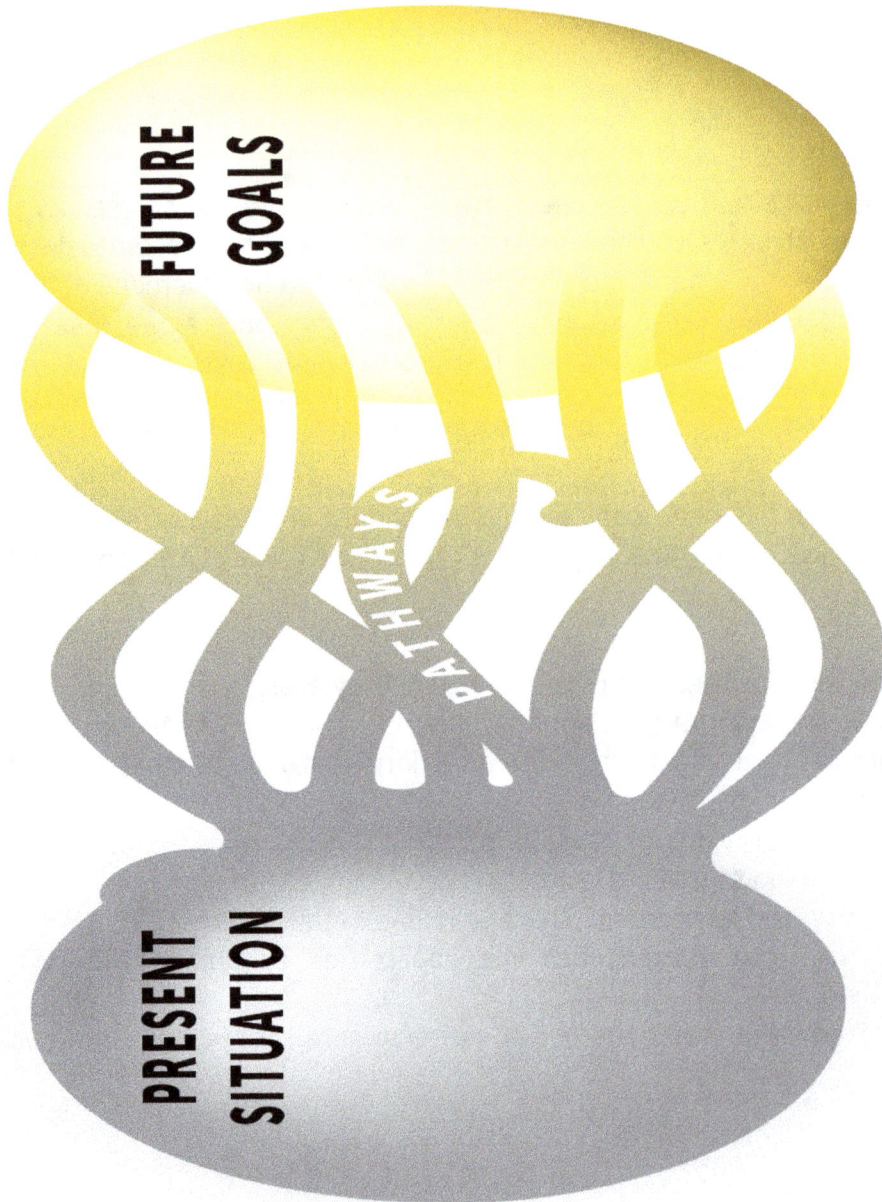

FUTURE GOALS

PATHWAYS

PRESENT SITUATION

# ~ SECTION 15 ~

## COACHING

# ☑ ADOPT

## COACHING IN THE CLASSROOM

Teachers in the classroom move between **four roles**: Teaching, Managing, Befriending (enhancing relationships), and Coaching. The behaviours that they choose in each of the roles are cognitively quite distinct from each other.

| Teaching | In this role teachers are informing, instructing, training, tutoring, explaining, demonstrating and educating. |
|---|---|
| Managing | In this role teachers are directing, controlling, leading, organising, supervising, commanding and attempting to compel. |
| Befriending | In this role teachers are establishing supportive relationships, encouraging, caring about, guiding, assisting and championing. |
| Coaching | In this role teachers are guiding, promoting, suggesting options, conversing, counselling, advising, encouraging, offering choices. |

However, in practice, the roles often overlap with each other or even merge, but it is always helpful to be clear about which role you intend to adopt as 'situations' emerge.

All four roles are important to us when we are teaching students to manage themselves responsibly. We will always be teaching and befriending. However, when we are encouraging students to self-manage, the emphasis on the other two roles shifts radically:

**We should always attempt to do less managing and more coaching.**

In the coaching role, we are supporting the student's emerging capability to manage themselves, make responsible choices, and take charge of their own learning and achievement.

**Coaching is the preferred role to choose when we are supporting the student's self-managing agenda.**

## 15.1
## ☑ ADOPT

### REPLACE RESCUING WITH COACHING

Sometimes teachers say to me: 'I don't have time to use the coaching questions. It's quicker to just show the student what to do.' However, if that is our habitual practice, we are teaching students to rely on the teacher every time a task seems hard.

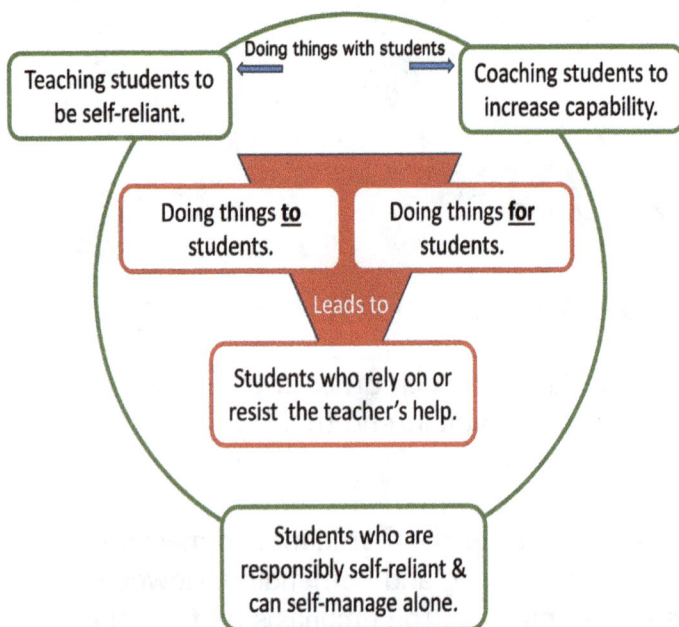

Doing things with students

Teaching students to be self-reliant. ← → Coaching students to increase capability.

Doing things **to** students.    Doing things **for** students.

Leads to

Students who rely on or resist the teacher's help.

Students who are responsibly self-reliant & can self-manage alone.

Instead of strengthening capability by 'helping', we can inadvertently promote dependency.

In the diagram, the teacher behaviours **in the triangle**[1] can promote helpless attitudes. When students come to believe that they need help to produce high-quality work, and when they come to rely upon their teachers or parents to provide that help, they tend to regard themselves as relatively helpless.

[1] Adapted from 'The Karpman Drama Triangle' (Stephen Karpman) and 'The Circle of Strength' (Shirley Brierly)

190

On the other hand, the behaviours **on the circle**[1] are empowering. Teaching self-management and using coaching processes have a positive effect on a student's self-reliance, self-efficacy, and resilience.

Instead of looking for help outside themselves, students learn to search inside themselves for the capabilities that they need. This is what coaching does. The coaching process uses questions to help students identify what they know and can do, and to work out new options and pathways when they get stuck.

This may seem simple, but the effects can be profound. In his work on attribution styles, Martin Seligman[2] demonstrated that students who learn to associate their success with internal events and believe that they can depend on their own capabilities tend to be self-reliant and resilient.

Coaching in the classroom is identified by the use of questions that help students when they are uncertain, get stuck or need encouragement. For example, 'Let me show you', or 'Do this' are replaced by: 'What have you done so far?', 'What have you tried?', 'What do you need to do to move forward?', 'What have you tried before in this situation?', 'What else could you do?'

Of course, there are times when either teaching or mentoring is needed. When the student has nothing to call on in their repertoire of behaviours, it is important to assist them to work out a way forward. However, whenever something is within the student's capability, coaching helps them with the confidence to rely on their own abilities.

Even in a situation where we suspect we will have to re-teach some material to a student, taking the few seconds to ask: 'What have you tried so far?' or 'Where are you getting stuck?' will both respect what the student has already attempted and give you a focus for any new teaching.

When in doubt about whether to step in and rescue a student who is struggling or to be a coach instead, give yourself this advice. Never do anything **FOR** a student that they are capable of doing for themselves! When you want to do something **WITH** a student that will extend their capabilities, use coaching as your primary tool.

---

[2] Martin Seligman: 'Learned Optimism'1990.

## 15.2

### ☑ ADOPT

#### USE A COACHING PROCESS

It is most useful for students when teachers adopt a recognised coaching process, rather than trust their intuition when they begin to adopt coaching in the classroom.

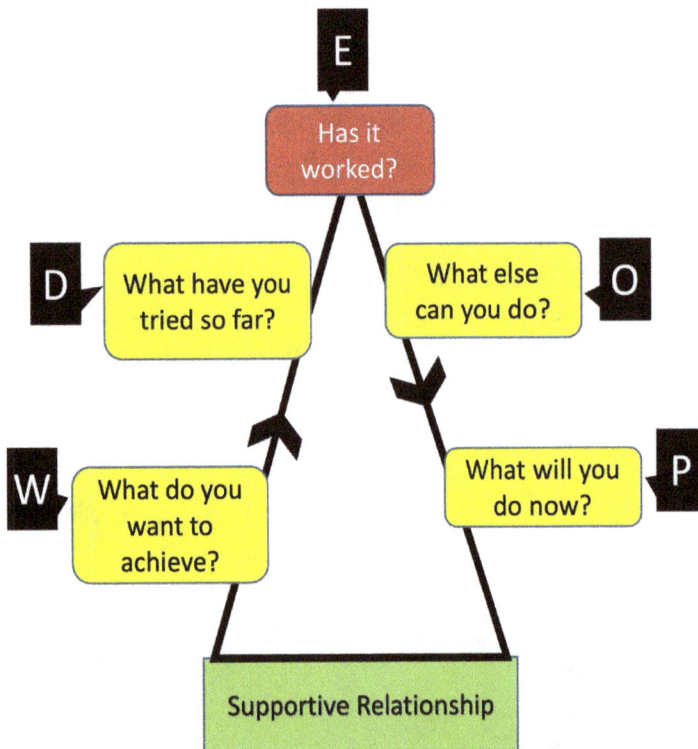

The WDEOP coaching procedures that I recommend are based on 'Reality Therapy'.[3] Although it was developed as a therapeutic process, it is a 5-step solution-focused procedure that has many applications.

The essential foundation is a productive and supportive relationship.

The five questions for which we can use the acronym WDEOP lead the student through a reflective process that mimics the way the mind works.

E — Has it worked?
D — What have you tried so far?
O — What else can you do?
W — What do you want to achieve?
P — What will you do now?

Supportive Relationship

W (**What do you WANT?**) helps the student to be clear about where they are stuck or what they want to achieve.
D (**What have you been DOING?**) asks them to identify progress so far.
E (**The EVALUATION question**) is the crucial question that generates the energy for creative thinking.
O (**What else can you do?**) invites the student to explore other **options**.

---

[3] Reality Therapy is a helping process developed by Dr William Glasser. Based on 'Choice Theory', this process is simple, helpful, and effective and can be adapted easily for the classroom.

**P (What next?)** leads the student to make a **plan** to implement other options.

As you begin to adopt the practice of coaching students, you will develop a repertoire of your own natural-sounding questions such as the ones suggested in the illustration below. However, it is a good idea to retain the general shape and sequence of the HWDEOP questioning process below so that it becomes familiar to the students. The goal is to encourage the students to accept the coaching questions as a natural way of thinking through an issue or problem, to the point where they will intuitively coach themselves whenever they need to.

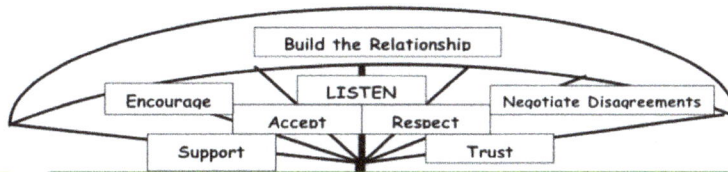

| | |
|---|---|
| **H** | How are you going? What's happening? Where are you up to? Are you seeing a problem? Where are you stuck? What is not working out? What's going well and what is not? What is your self-talk? Do you need a coach? |
| **W** | What would you like to achieve? How do you want things to go? What's the next step? If things were working out, what would be happening? What's your immediate goal? Where do you want to go with this? What do you want next? |
| **D** | What are you doing at the present? Can you tell me what you have tried? Where are you stuck? What are you thinking? What have you tried that has taken you forward? Is anything that you are doing helping? What are you feeling? |
| **E** | Is it working so far? Is what you have tried working at all? Are you going forward or backwards? Has anything worked? Are you moving forward? Are you making any progress when you do that? Will it work out if you keep going this way? |
| **O** | What else could you do? Is there another way to approach this? Have you any other ideas? What would be a completely different way to approach this? What have you done to 'unstick' yourself in the past? What would Einstein have tried? |
| **P** | Which ideas are you going to try? Will you use S.M.A.R.T. ? What specifically are you going to try? How will you know that you are making progress? Does that sound good to you? Is it realistic? When will you start? |

When students habituate this kind of thinking, they can apply it to direct their learning, and also contribute this coaching capability to the collaborative effectiveness of the class.

## 15.3

☑ **ADOPT**

### COACHING TO ENCOURAGE SELF-DIRECTED LEARNING

One of the signs that students are **not** self-managing is that they put their hand up and ask for help as soon as they are stuck. They shift the responsibility for their progress back to the teacher.

When students are self-managing and directing their own learning they make an effort to get past the problem before they ask for help.

As we introduce coaching as a key classroom tool, it's helpful to work with the students to clarify the responsibilities in the classroom.

**The teacher** is responsible for instruction and for communicating the content and processes that are prescribed by the curriculum.

**The teacher** is also responsible for demonstrations of any of the skills required, and for setting up activities that will enable the students to practise.

**The teacher** then steps back from being 'the sage on the stage' and becomes 'the guide on the side'! They pick up the role of friend (to encourage) and coach (to help students take control of their own learning).

**The students** are responsible for setting their own goals and for asking questions when they don't understand or need clarification.

**The students** are responsible for directing their own learning by asking themselves these questions:
- What do I want to achieve with the work I am doing in this class or subject?
- How much effort am I prepared to make to achieve what I want?

It's always useful to remind students that **they can achieve what they want provided they are willing to pay the price in time and effort.**

**The students** are responsible for asking for the assistance of a coach **after** they have asked themselves at least the first four coaching questions:

- What do I want?
- What am I doing to achieve what I want?
- Is anything I am doing working?
- Is there anything else I can try?

If they are not moving forward after these self-coaching questions, then is the time to ask for the teacher to step into the role of coach.

As students become used to this division of responsibilities, they will habitually take charge of their own learning and achievement.

## 15.4
## ☑ ADOPT

### ENCOURAGE PEER COACHING

As teachers use coaching in the classroom, they will inevitably introduce students to the possibility of coaching each other.

Like so many of the other transformative effects of teaching students to manage themselves, introducing the skills needed for peer coaching, and encouraging students to coach each other, pay back the time that you invest in it.

Instead of being the harried teacher, attempting to service the enquiries and requests for support from the class, you can become the director of coaching services in the classroom. This is not exploitation of the time of the most capable students, but a way of enhancing their learning.

Let me give you an example:

> Anne was allocated a Year 9 Maths class with an extraordinarily wide range of student abilities. Probably because of her reputation as an exceptional teacher, she was asked to take on a class that had six or seven students with learning disabilities, several students who told anyone who would listen that they hated maths, and several very capable high-achieving students who easily got bored.

It was clear that this class of 30 would be a challenge. Anne decided from the start that using conventional teaching practices would not work. She told one of her colleagues: "This class really needs five different teachers!"

As soon as she said those words aloud, the solution struck her. She needed to recruit her students to be teachers and coaches. She created individual competency charts for each student. (It was a very traditional school, so these competencies were mostly based on chapter completion in the textbook.) She taught mini-lessons to small groups when they were ready to tackle the next competency on their chart: there was no point in 'teaching to the middle' in this class.

Most importantly, she taught the coaching process to **all** the students. Every student was expected to be able to coach any other student. Initially, she noticed that some of the faster learners tended to do the work of the people they were coaching, so she explained how important it was to coach but not 'rescue'. By the end of Week 3, the students were way behind on the maths curriculum, but most were becoming confident coaches!

Anne did get some early signs of success. She noticed that one of the twin boys who rarely did any work in other classes was coaching his sibling, and that both were completing the work on their competency charts!

She worried about Aaron, her most capable student, who was such a popular coach that he did not seem to be doing much of his own work - even though he reassured her that he was way ahead on his competency chart. Anne was anxious about what Aaron's mother would say at the parent-teacher meeting in Week 7. She was delighted when Aaron's mum's first words were: "What have you done with Aaron? He is enjoying maths for the first time in years. He has always been good at it, but usually said it was boring. Now, most evenings he has his head in his maths textbook, telling me he has to get ahead so that he can coach other students."

Anne's most telling feedback came (in a backhanded way) from the Head of Maths after the mid-semester tests. He took her aside and asked if she had 'taught the students the answers' to the test questions. He could not believe that all the students in this diverse and potentially difficult class had done so well on the test!

Teaching students to be coaches usually has all the benefits that are illustrated in Anne's story:

- Students persevere with a task longer because they know that they will be coached rather than rescued.
- Students adopt the coaching process as a way of thinking for themselves.
- Students understand that they are expected to manage their own learning.
- The students who accept responsibility and have learned to self-manage capably are able to use their coaching skills to model for others, and to influence their classmates to adopt higher levels of self-management.

# ~ SECTION 16 ~

## CONCLUSION

I am writing this in a time of teacher shortage. After decades of taking teachers for granted, society has suddenly found that we are not easy to replace! The nonsense about 'long holidays' is giving way to recognition of the intensity and complexity of teachers' work.

William Glasser[1] wrote that effective teaching might be the hardest work there is. It may well be – and if it is, then there need to be some changes that make the work less overwhelming and more rewarding. The 'ill-being'[2] that sometimes seems to permeate many classes and schools will have to be transformed into wellbeing. The 101 strategies that fill the pages of this book are intended to contribute to the changes required.

These initiatives will contribute to a better future for teachers and teaching, and the changes will come from the teachers and how they work. 'Fixes' to education from 'the outside' usually make things worse! If teaching is to become the attractive profession it deserves to be, teachers will have to initiate the changes that are needed.

It is no wonder that far too many teachers can become disillusioned when many of the strategies that they use are based on a psychology that is long past its

---

[1] William Glasser MD. 'Schools without Failure' 1975.

[2] Edward L. Deci and Richard Ryan Deci characterise 'ill-being' as the opposite of wellbeing. 'Self-Determination Theory and the Facilitation of Intrinsic Motivation, Social Development, and Well-being'. American Psychologist, 2000.

use-by date; when strategies are not systematically taught in teacher training; when so many teachers base their strategies on what they observed from their own teachers. And yet.......

...... And yet in every school I have worked in, there have been teachers who have used and taught me the strategies that can be found in this book. Teachers whose classrooms were happy, interesting places; places where students were at their best. Knowledge about what works to promote wellbeing in the classroom is already available - if we seek it!

Let me digress for a moment:

*In my teenage years, I was told this story - by a teacher of course! It's the story of a man who sent his two servants into the desert telling them to fill their pockets with all the diamonds they would find.*

*One of the men knew that the errand was foolish. "Everyone knows that there are no diamonds in the desert", he muttered to himself. He returned to his master with pockets full of pebbles. "I did my best," he explained, "but there was nothing to find but these worthless stones."*

*The second servant searched until dark. As night fell, he came upon patch after patch of shiny stones. He filled the pockets of his clothes with as many as he could carry. Staggering home, he unloaded for his master pocket after pocket of glittering diamonds. "I did my best", he explained, "but this was all that I could carry."*

I took a lot from that story in my early years as a teacher. It helped me to understand the variety of perceptions among my new colleagues – and the different attitudes that flowed from those perceptions. Some teachers I was working with saw themselves as the critical factor in student learning. They believed every student was capable and would flourish with the right teaching. They were uncut diamonds waiting to be polished. If their students were struggling, they tried to extend the repertoire of their practices so that the work was more inviting, more challenging, and more accessible to the students they were teaching. They knew that when their efforts were not yet working, they could do something different – and they did! Others around them did not change because they did not know what else to do - and were too proud to learn from their colleagues!

*My first teaching position was in a 'Secondary Modern' school in northern England. It was a tough beginning. Truancy was high. Poverty soured the community. Most of my colleagues were working hard but drowning in the tide of negativity created by a Principal and his Deputy, Harold, who between them orchestrated a bullying culture that might have come from a Charles Dickens story. It was a grey place. I was doing my best, but quickly losing heart.*

*Somewhere towards the end of Term One, I came across Hedley. A tall, stooped, intense man, he never came to the staffroom. I passed him occasionally in the corridor clutching musical instruments and hurrying into classrooms where young people waited expectantly. Enquiring about this enigmatic figure, I learned little from my colleagues until one cheerful person took me aside and told me: "Two things you need to know about Hedley. The kids love him. The tyrants ignore him! Most of us are too scared to take sides."*

*In Term Two, Hedley stopped to talk to me: "Concert. In the Hall. Wednesday lunchtime. I think you will enjoy it. I hope I will see you there." He darted off.*

*At the time appointed, I was a bit bemused to find myself following a huge crowd of students into the assembly hall. Truth to tell I was a bit apprehensive to see that there were only a few teachers present. School assemblies in that place usually required every teacher to attend, all doing our best to quieten the sea of restlessness while Harold bellowed for silence, but as usual never quite achieved it!*

*This was entirely different. The musicians were not on the stage but grouped in the middle of the floor: thirty or so with instruments and the rest in bright clothing. Hedley stood among them and tapped with a conductor's baton on a rickety lectern. The result was astonishing to me. There were probably four hundred students arranged around the performers, some sitting, many standing. All of them became suddenly silent.*

*A small girl announced that we would hear pieces from a brand-new musical called 'Joseph and His Amazing Technicolor Dreamcoat.*[3] *For 30 minutes we were spellbound by performances that brought tears to my eyes. I am no musician, but the production seemed magical to me. The audience, that same audience that caused so much aggravation in an ordinary school assembly, listened with rapt attention. The applause was warm, appreciative, never raucous. These students were being their best selves because they understood that they were being invited to be their best!*

That experience prepared me for a lifetime of teaching and leading teachers. In every school I have worked in, there have been teachers like Hedley: teachers who looked for the best in students and found what they expected. I have seen it as my job to cultivate these 'diamonds', to recognise and grow the positivity, wellbeing and enthusiasm being nurtured by the teachers who had these things in common:

- Whoever was in their class, they set out to establish productive relationships with them.
- They established boundaries that were clearly understood and guarded them with calm assertiveness.
- They taught the students how to behave well, and how to manage their own behaviour.
- They expected students to do their best and set up the learning in ways that enabled the young people to rise to that expectation.
- They showed unconditional respect to the young people they taught, whether it was deserved or not.
- When things went wrong (as they did) they simply picked up the pieces and started again.

Years later, when I learned Choice Theory, I understood why students behave so differently with teachers like these. Through learning this insightful explanation of human behaviour and motivation, it is easy to see why coercive environments discourage students from taking responsibility, while calm, caring classrooms bring out the best in students. I have tried to pass on an understanding of this theory as widely as possible. **But it is not the theory alone that makes a difference!**

---

[3] I only later found out that this musical by Andrew Lloyd Webber and Tim Rice was very new and musically quite experimental.

## THE DIFFERENCES THAT MAKE A DIFFERENCE ARE THE STRATEGIES THAT FLOW FROM THE THEORY.

The teachers whose classrooms nurture both student and teacher wellbeing **do** understand what motivates and what discourages young people. However, they promote self-management in the classroom because they have more than knowledge; they have the practices that accompany their insights. They don't just expect responsible behaviour, **they teach it**.

Almost every teacher I have worked with began their career with the same 'big idea': they wanted to be the best teacher they could be and to earn the appreciation of their students.

However, what the teachers who have held on to their dream know is that 'big ideas' have to be matched by a sizable (and ever-growing) repertoire of strategies.

**The brain**, the source of humanity's ability to transcend its natural limitations, offers us a model for wellness and resilience in the classroom: for enduring professional satisfaction.

Every great idea and every powerful action that emanates from the brain begins with the connection of two neurons. Then, as more and more brain cells are connected, the resulting schemas generate the ideas and actions that enhance our human experience.

In the same way, the foundation of effective teaching is the adoption of simple but profoundly effective strategies – and then extending our repertoire. What we learn from one strategy or process leads us to another. As we focus those strategies on helping young people to manage themselves well and to get the best from themselves, the impossible burden of trying to force students to do what is painful for them because we want them to do it disappears.

My intention in writing this book was to offer you access to a repertoire of strategies that will promote self-management in your classroom. My inspiration for writing the book has been the legions of teachers who already use these strategies; those who teach young people to manage themselves and to take responsibility for the only person whom they can control – themselves!

202

## What if:

*What if* just one teacher were to take the strategies in this book and use them to change the experience of the students in their class?

*What if* the students in that teacher's class were to learn how to manage themselves so well that their life, their relationships, and their future happiness would be enriched by that learning?

*What if* that teacher were you?

# Acknowledgments

This book could not have been completed without the erudite assistance of my wife Valerie who has been my editor, proofreader, and much more. She has kept me firmly on task when I was inclined to procrastinate and gave me encouragement whenever I needed it.

A big 'thank you' also to Mark Asher, John Archibald, Aminta Miller, and Emma Kennedy who gave me feedback on the rough drafts of the book and made many helpful and practical suggestions to improve the text.

Thank you to all the inspirational teachers with whom I have worked and who already use the strategies described in this book. They are too numerous to mention individually, but their work on behalf of young people deserves warm appreciation.

Finally, thank you to the faculty members of Glasser Australia and William Glasser International who are my colleagues in teaching the liberating psychology of internal control on which this book is grounded.

# Appendix 1

# Teaching Students to Self-Manage in the Classroom
## Detailed Index

RELATIONSHIPS